A Citizens Theatre Production

The Libertine

by **Stephen Jeffreys**

This production was first performed at the Citizens Theatre, Glasgow, on 3 May 2014

Performances at the Citizens Theatre:
3–24 May 2014

Performances at Bristol Old Vic:
28–31 May 2014

The original production of *The Libertine* was presented by Out of Joint at the University of Warwick Arts Centre on 20 October 1994 and then on tour culminating at the Royal Court Theatre, London, on 6 December 1994.

The Libertine

by **Stephen Jeffreys**

Cast

Billy Downs	**Charlie Archer**
Charles Sackville/Harry Harris	**Andy Clark**
George Etherege/ Jacob Huysmans	**Tony Cownie**
Charles II	**John Hodgkinson**
John Wilmot, 2nd Earl of Rochester	**Martin Hutson**
Elizabeth Malet	**Lucianne McEvoy**
Tom Alcock	**Lee Mengo**
Mrs Will Ufton/Molly Luscombe	**Barbara Rafferty**
Elizabeth Barry	**Gillian Saker**
Jane	**Elexi Walker**

With **Pearl Appleby**, **Liam Harkins**, **Amy McGregor**, **Jack Mullen** and **Loretta Scott**

Creative Team

Director	**Dominic Hill**
Designer	**Tom Piper**
Lighting Designer	**Lizzie Powell**
Composer	**Hilary Brooks**
Movement Director	**Kally Lloyd-Jones**
Assistant Director	**Danielle McIlven**
Fight Director	**EmmaClaire Brightlyn**
Sound Designer	**Guy Coletta**
Casting Director	**Camilla Evans CDG**

Introduction

It's now twenty years since the premiere of *The Libertine* at Warwick Arts Centre in Max Stafford-Clark's production. In that time the play has enjoyed numerous reincarnations; an American premiere by Chicago's Steppenwolf with John Malkovich in the lead in a production by Terry Johnson; a radio version directed by the much-missed Claire Grove with Bill Nighy; a film directed by Laurence Dunmore starring Johnny Depp; a reading to celebrate the fiftieth anniversary of the English Stage Company at the Royal Court Theatre starring Kevin McNally; and numerous drama-school productions of which the ones at Mountview Theatre School have been the most notable.

So the Second Earl of Rochester has flitted in and out of my life all this time and my fictionalisation of him has changed with time and circumstances. Dominic Hill's revival at the Glasgow Citizens Theatre (the first professional production in Britain since the Out of Joint original) has provided me with an opportunity to arrive at a new edition which I can finally regard as definitive.

Two factors were influential in making the journey such a slow one. The first was purely personal: while I was writing the second half of the play in 1994, my mother died and the consequent loss of focus in my life was reflected in my organisation of the material.

The second factor was a result of the abundance of incident in my subject's life. Though Rochester was dead at thirty-three, he was involved in many more incidents than can be fitted into a single play. But even though I didn't dramatise his abduction of a wealthy heiress, his involvement in two battles at sea and his career as a reluctant duellist, I couldn't resist including in the first production the episode where, as a means of escaping the King's attentions, he posed successfully for several weeks as a quack doctor in the East End. It was after an early preview of the Steppenwolf production that John Malkovich pointed out to me that I was asking him to play a man in terminal physical decline who simultaneously turns in an astoundingly energetic comic performance as the cod Italian Doctor Bendo. He asked for a new scene immediately and played it the very next evening. Without Doctor Bendo, the whole second half then fell into shape and it's this version, give or take a few interpolations from the film, that you can read here.

I would like to reiterate my thanks to Max Stafford-Clark, probably the greatest director of new plays the British theatre has ever seen, for commissioning *The Libertine* in the first place; and to the late Jeremy Lamb, one of Rochester's biographers, who communicated to me his passion for John Wilmot and all his work. Jeremy's life and death were appropriately Rochesterian.

Rochester was a man who was endowed with every conceivable talent and chose, deliberately and methodically, to waste each one. It is a response to life which still strikes a chord today.

Stephen Jeffreys
April 2014

Creative Team

STEPHEN JEFFREYS | WRITER

Stephen Jeffreys' plays include *The Libertine* and *I Just Stopped By to See the Man* (Royal Court); *Valued Friends* and *A Going Concern* (Hampstead); *Bugles at the Gates of Jalalabad* (part of the Tricycle Theatre's *Great Game* season about Afghanistan); *The Convicts' Opera* (Out of Joint); *Lost Land* (starring John Malkovich, Steppenwolf, Chicago); *The Art of War* (Sydney Theatre Company) and *A Jovial Crew* (RSC). His adaptation of Dickens' *Hard Times* has been performed all over the world. He wrote the films *The Libertine* (starring Johnny Depp) and *Diana* (starring Naomi Watts). He co-authored the Beatles musical *Backbeat* which opened at the Citizens Theatre and went on to seasons in London's West End, Toronto and Los Angeles. He recently translated *The Magic Flute* for English National Opera in Simon McBurney's production. For eleven years he was Literary Associate at the Royal Court Theatre where he is now a member of the Council. His celebrated playwriting workshops have influenced numerous writers.

DOMINIC HILL | DIRECTOR

Dominic Hill is Artistic Director of the Citizens Theatre. Since joining the Citizens in 2011, he has directed *Miss Julie*, *Crime and Punishment*, *Far Away*, *Seagulls*, *Doctor Faustus*, *Sleeping Beauty*, *Krapp's Last Tape*, *Footfalls*, *King Lear* and *Betrayal* (winner of Best Director, 2012 CATS Award). Before joining the Citizens he was Artistic Director of the Traverse Theatre in Edinburgh and Joint Artistic Director of Dundee Rep. Other credits include *Falstaff* and *Macbeth* (Scottish Opera) and *The City Madam* (RSC). He has directed in theatres in London and throughout the UK.

TOM PIPER | DESIGNER

As Associate Designer for the RSC, Tom has designed over thirty productions including *Much Ado About Nothing*, *Macbeth*, *City Madam*, *The Histories Cycle* (for which he won the 2009 Olivier Award for Best Costume Design and was nominated for Best Set Design), *As You Like It*, *The Grain Store*, *Hamlet*, *A Midsummer Night's Dream* and *Antony and Cleopatra*. Other recent designs include *Vera Vera Vera* (Royal Court); *Richard III*, *The Tempest*, *As You Like It* (Bridge Project BAM/Old Vic); *Zorro* (West End/tour/Paris/Moscow/Amsterdam/Atlanta/Tokyo); *Dealer's Choice* (Menier Chocolate Factory/West End); *Falstaff*, *Macbeth* (Scottish Opera); *Fall* (RSC/Traverse); *Red Velvet* (Tricycle/St Ann's Warehouse, New York); *Bracken Moor* (Tricycle/Shared Experience); *The Plough and the Stars*, *The Crucible*, *Six Characters in Search of an Author* (Abbey, Dublin); *The Big Meal* (Bath) and *King Lear* (Citizens Theatre).

LIZZIE POWELL | LIGHTING DESIGNER

Lizzie trained at London Academy of Music and Dramatic Arts. Her lighting designs for the Citizens Theatre are *Far Away, Seagulls, Krapp's Last Tape, Footfalls*. Other theatre work includes *Glasgow Girls, In Time O' Strife, My Shrinking Life, Enquirer, An Appointment with the Wicker Man, Knives in Hens, Girl X, Mary Queen of Scots Got Her Head Chopped Off, Our Teacher's a Troll, Venus As A Boy* (NTS), *Debuts* (NTS with Traverse); *Woyzeck, A Streetcar Named Desire, Show 3, Glitterland, A Series of Impossible Tasks* (Secret Theatre, Lyric Hammersmith); *Weekly Rep* (Royal Court); *Any Given Day, While You Lie, The Dark Things* (Traverse); *First Light* (Imaginate Festival); *Pangaa* (Ankur Productions); *Treasure Island* (Wee Stories); *Huxley's Lab, Spring Awakening* (Grid Iron/Lung Ha's); *Caged, Pobby and Dingan, The Book of Beasts* (Catherine Wheels); *Under Milk Wood* (Theatre Royal, Northampton); *The Wasp Factory* (Cumbernauld Theatre); *The Wall* (Tron); *Great Expectations* (Byre Theatre/Prime Productions); *Making History* (Ouroboros) and *Travels With My Aunt* (New Wolsey).

HILARY BROOKS | COMPOSER

Hilary is a Glasgow-based composer, musical director/arranger and pianist. MD credits include: *Dare to Care* (Stellar Quines); *Glasgow Girls* (NTS/Citizens/Theatre Royal Stratford East); *White Christmas* (Pitlochry Festival Theatre); *Sweeney Todd: The Demon Barber of Fleet Street, Sunshine on Leith, Gypsy, Nightflights, Cabaret* (Dundee Rep); *The Rink* (Belgrade Theatre, Coventry); *The Prime of Miss Jean Brodie, Alice* (Royal Lyceum, Edinburgh). Composer credits include: *James and the Giant Peach* (Citizens Theatre); *Memory of Water* (Stellar Quines); *The Eastern Bride* (Kharis Productions); *Nightflights* (Dundee Rep); *Meeting Matthew* (Òran Mór); *Beauty and the Beast* (Byre, St Andrews); *Der Golem* (GFT); *F.O.T., Mr Wymi, Salut Serge* (BBC Worldwide). Hilary is co-founder of *PianoPiano* with the composer Karen MacIver. Their debut album *Dedicated* features nine original tracks performed by the composers on two grand pianos. '*Two great musicians, blending their virtuosity with tales of nine iconic women… a unique and landmark recording.*' *Musician* Magazine.

KALLY LLOYD-JONES | MOVEMENT DIRECTOR

Kally Lloyd-Jones trained as a dancer, has an MA in English Literature and Film Studies from Glasgow University and has worked as a director, choreographer, dancer, movement director and teacher in the UK and internationally. She is founder and Artistic Director of Company Chordelia and has recently created, directed and toured the company's productions *Dance Derby, Les Amoureux, Cabaret Chordelia, Miranda* and *The Seven Deadly Sins*, an award-winning co-production with Scottish Opera. Her choreography/movement direction credits include Scottish

Opera, The Royal Conservatoire of Scotland, Tête a Tête Opera, Edinburgh International Festival, Ankur Productions, King's Theatre Glasgow, Traverse Theatre, Licketyspit Theatre Company and the Citizens Theatre. Directing credits include Scottish Opera, RCS, The Byre, Tête a Tête Opera Festival, Bloomsbury Opera and St Andrew's Opera.

DANIELLE McILVEN | ASSISTANT DIRECTOR

Danielle is currently on the Theatre Directing MFA at Birkbeck, University of London. During her placement at the Citizens Theatre she has assisted on *Crime and Punishment*, *Scarfed for Life*, *The Jungle Book*, *Miss Julie* and *The Libertine*.

EMMACLAIRE BRIGHTLYN | FIGHT DIRECTOR

EmmaClaire is a Scottish-Canadian actress and Fight Director. Recent credits include: *Dragon* (NTS/Vox Motus/National Theatre of China); *Macbeth* (Perth/Tron); *Private Lives* (Òran Mór). For the Citizens Theatre (as Fight Consultant): *The Maids*, *Takin' Over the Asylum*, *Miss Julie*. She was also an Assistant Fight Director and Fight Captain for the arena show *Ben Hur Live* in Rome, Italy.

GUY COLETTA | SOUND DESIGNER

Guy studied at the SAE Institute Glasgow. His previous shows include, *Miss Julie*, *The Jungle Book*, *The Maids* (Citizens Theatre); *Sleeping Beauty*, *King Lear* (Sound No1); *Leaving Planet Earth* (Grid Iron); *Black Watch* (2013); *Glasgow Girls* (2012/2014) and *Appointment with the Wicker Man* (NTS/Sound No2).

CAMILLA EVANS CDG | CASTING DIRECTOR

Camilla is currently working alongside Maggie Lunn on *A Streetcar Named Desire* and *The Crucible* (Old Vic). Recent theatre includes: *War Horse* (West End); *Jane Eyre* (Bristol Old Vic); *To Sir, With Love* (UK tour); *Say it With Flowers* (Sherman); *Doctor Faustus* (WYP/Citizens). TV: *Hustle* series 7 and 8 (BBC).

Cast

CHARLIE ARCHER | BILLY DOWNS

Recent theatre credits include: *Billy Budd* (Southwark Playhouse/Secret/Heart) nominated for Best Male Off-West End Award; *A Midsummer Night's Dream* (Royal & Derngate); Mark Rylance's *Pop-up Shakespeare* (Shakespeare's Globe); *Ladybird* (New Diorama); *The Illusion* (Southwark Playhouse); *The Band* (Soho); *Bunny's Vendetta* (The Glassworks); *Crows On The Wire* (Blue Eagle Productions).

ANDY CLARK | CHARLES SACKVILLE / HARRY HARRIS

Recent theatre credits include: *Of Mice and Men* (West Yorkshire Playhouse); *Gastronauts* (Royal Court); *I'm With the Band* (Traverse/Wales Millennium Theatre); *Time and the Conways* (Dundee Rep/Royal Lyceum, Edinburgh); *The Strange Undoing of Prudencia Hart* (NTS); *The Government Inspector* (Communicado/Tron); *Ya Beauty and the Beast* (Tron); *Othello, The Wizard of Oz, Hamlet* (Citizens Theatre); *Measure for Measure* (Clwyd Theatr Cymru); *Vernon God Little* (Young Vic); *Decky Does a Bronco* (Grid Iron). **TV credits include:** *Rubenesque* (Kudos/Pirate); *River City* (BBC Scotland) *Rebus* (SMG). **Film credits include:** *The Da Vinci Code* (Rose Line Productions). **Radio credits include:** *The Five of Spades, Rebus, The Dead Hour, The Whole of the Moon* (BBC Radio 4).

TONY COWNIE | GEORGE ETHEREGE / JACOB HUYSMANS

Recent theatre credits include: *Union* (Royal Lyceum, Edinburgh) and *King Lear* (Citizens Theatre). Tony has directed some twenty-six productions for The Lyceum, including *Long Day's Journey Into Night, A Taste of Honey, Educating Agnes, Romeo and Juliet, The Cherry Orchard, The Beauty Queen of Leenane, Mrs Warren's Profession* (co-production with Nottingham Playhouse). **Other directing credits include**: *Backpacker Blues* (Òran Mór); *The Woman Who Cooked Her Husband* (tour); *The Laird O' Grippy* (Dundee Rep); the Herald Angel–winning *Empty Jesters* (Traverse); *Tutti Frutti* (NTS).

JOHN HODGKINSON | CHARLES II

Recent theatre credits include: *Donkeys' Years* (Rose, Kingston); *Unscorched* (Papatango); *A Walk on Part* (Soho/Arts/Live, Newcastle); *Onassis* (West End); *Hapgood* (Birmingham Rep/West Yorkshire Playhouse); *Absurdia* (Donmar Warehouse). **Recent TV credits include:** *Big Bad World* (Paramount); *The Escape Artist*, *Silk*, *Criminal Justice*, *Holby City* (BBC); *Whitechapel* (ITV); *Peep Show* (Channel 4). **Recent film credits include:** *Heart of Lightness* (Jan Vardøen); *Leave to Remain* (Bruce Goodison); *Skyfall* (Sam Mendes).

MARTIN HUTSON | ROCHESTER

Theatre credits include: *If Only* (Chichester); *Thursday* (ETT/Brink); *Antony and Cleopatra* (Chichester/Liverpool Playhouse); *Butley*, *Ghosts* (Ian Charleson Award nomination), *Another Country* (West End); *The Heart of Robin Hood*, *As You Like It*, *Titus Andronicus* (RSC); *Taking Sides*, *Collaboration* (Chichester/West End); *The Voysey Inheritance*, *The Mandate* (National Theatre); *The Rubenstein Kiss* (Hampstead); *As You Like It* (Ian Charleson Award nomination), *The Comedy of Errors* (Sheffield Crucible); *The Rivals* (Bristol Old Vic); *The Jew of Malta* (Almeida); *Hamlet* (Birmingham Rep/Elsinor Castle); *Five Finger Exercise* (Salisbury Playhouse). **TV credits include:** *The Honourable Woman* (BBC/Sundance); *A Very British Sex Scandal* (Channel 4); *The Passion* (BBC/HBO); *Foyles War* (Greenlit); *Midsomer Murders* (Bentley). **Film credits include:** *Atonement* (Working Title); *Virtual Sexuality* (Virtual Sexuality Films); *Who Gets the Dog?* (Company Pictures).

LUCIANNE McEVOY | ELIZABETH MALET

Lucianne was born in Dublin and trained at the Samuel Beckett Centre, Trinity College, graduating in 1999 with a distinction. Since then she has worked in the UK and Ireland with companies including National Theatre of Scotland, Grid Iron, Òran Mór, Theatre Babel, Royal Lyceum, Edinburgh, Corcadorca (Cork), The Abbey Theatre (Dublin), English Touring Theatre, Out of Joint and National Theatre. Lucianne has performed in various radio plays and works regularly as a voiceover artist. **TV credits include:** Tara in NY-LON for Channel Four (2004). Lucianne has been based in Glasgow since 2011.

LEE MENGO | TOM ALCOCK

Recent theatre credits include: *6:37* (Royal Court); *It's a Family Affair* (Sherman); *Spangled,* (Theatre Critics of Wales nomination; Mercury Theatre Wales); *Accidental Death of an Anarchist, The Hired Man* (Torch); *Grapes of Wrath, The Voyage, Mabinogion* (Clwyd Theatr Cymru); *Whole Truth* (Latitude Festival); *Muscle* (Roxy); *Macbeth* (PAC); *Richard III, Canterbury Tales, Moll Flanders* (Mappa Mundi); *The Bells of Shoreditch* (Dirty Protest); *The Bankrupt Bride* (Greenwich); *A Child's Christmas In Wales* (Theatre Na' Nog). **Recent TV credits include**: *Stella,* series 1 & 2 (Sky); *The Indian Doctor* series 1, 2 & 3 (BBC); *Skins* (E4); *D Plates, Gwaith Cartref* (S4C). **Recent film credits include:** *One Chance* (Weinstein Company); *High Tide* (Long Arm Films); *The Hours* (Stray Bison). Lee has recorded numerous radio plays for BBC Radio 4 and Radio Wales.

BARBARA RAFFERTY | MOLLY LUSCOMBE / MRS WILL UFTON

Barbara studied at the Sorbonne Paris and RSAMD (now Royal Conservatoire of Scotland). She has performed in theatres all over Britain. She played Maggie in Giles Havergal's Citizens Theatre production of *Men Should Weep* (1998) and more recently as Mom in *True West* (2013). **Recent theatre credits include:** *The House of Bernarda Alba* (Tramway); *Blood Wedding* (Donmar Warehouse); *Steel Magnolias* (Dundee Rep); *The Missing* (NTS); two tours of the London Palladium Production of *Chitty Chitty Bang Bang* and many pantomimes at the King's Theatre in Glasgow. **Television credits include**: *Rab C Nesbitt* as Ella Cotter (The Comedy Unit), *Rockface, River City, Sea of Souls, Garrow's Law, Doctors, Murder Rooms* (BBC); *Taggart* (STV). **Film credits include**: *Blood Red Roses* (Blood Red Roses Productions); *Last King of Scotland* (Fox Searchlight Pictures); *Women Talking Dirty* (Rocket Productions); *Billy Bongo Leaves Home* (Peel Street Films); *Last Word* (Sigma Films); *The Wicker Man* (British Lion Films). She has recorded many radio plays and comedies. Barbara is married to actor Sean Scanlan.

GILLIAN SAKER | ELIZABETH BARRY

Gillian is a recent graduate of the Royal Welsh College of Music and Drama. **Recent theatre credits include**: *The River* (Royal Court); *Othello* (nominated for Best Female Off-West End Award; Riverside Studios) and *Stephen Ward* (Sydmonton Festival). **Recent TV credits include**: *Ripper Street* (BBC); *Misfits* (Clerkenwell/E4); *Law and Order: UK* (Kudos/ITV). **Film credits include:** *You're Ugly Too* (IFB/SP Films).

ELEXI WALKER | JANE

Recent theatre credits include: *The Jungle Book* (Citizens Theatre); *Europa* (ZKM, Croatia; Dresden Staatsschauspiel; Teatr Polski Bydgoszcz; Birmingham Rep); *You Can Still Make a Killing*, *The Taming of the Shrew* (Southwark Playhouse); *DNA* (Hull Truck Theatre/UK tour); *To Kill a Mockingbird* (York Theatre Royal); *The Vagina Monologues* (Mark Goucher Ltd., No. 1 tour). **TV and radio credits include**: *Doctors* (BBC Television); *Reality Check* (BBC Asian Network).

Citizens Theatre

'As theatrical icons go, few come bigger than Glasgow's Citizens Theatre' *Herald*

The Citizens Theatre is an iconic venue and theatre company based in the Gorbals area of Glasgow. It has been one of Scotland's flagship producing theatres since 1945, recognised internationally as a leader in its field. Fondly known as The Citz, it is led by Artistic Director, Dominic Hill.

Within a beautiful Victorian auditorium that dates from 1878, the Citizens presents a world-class, contemporary repertoire based on bold new interpretations of classic texts.

As our name suggests, we believe our work can enhance and transform the lives of citizens of all ages, cultures and social backgrounds. We believe that theatre and the arts have an essential role to play in bringing about positive social change and that creativity is at the heart of learning.

Every week of the year we provide a range of opportunities for people of all ages and backgrounds to get involved in the creative life of our theatre and develop skills and self-confidence in an inclusive environment where new friendships can flourish. We are passionate about everything we offer to children, young people, students, seniors and families. We work closely with people with additional support needs and those in disadvantaged and marginalised communities. Everyone is welcome to take part in our projects, classes and productions.

With the expertise of the many artists, writers and actors we collaborate with, our ambition is to provide unique and memorable cultural experiences for all.

For the latest information on all our shows, and to find out how you can take part, visit us online at **citz.co.uk**

Find us on Facebook: **citizenstheatre** | Follow us on Twitter **@citizenstheatre**

Citizens Theatre, 119 Gorbals Street, Glasgow, G5 9DS
0141 429 0022 | citz.co.uk

Registered Company No. SC022513
Scottish Charity No. SCO01337

The Citizens Company

Amy Angus
Drama Class Tutor

Jackie Arbuthnott
Drama Class Assistant

Tom Arnott
Front of House

Lorraine Barclay
Stage Door
Administrator

Isabella Basset
Front of House

Omar Bhatia
Front of House

David Black
Front of House

Emily Black
Wardrobe Assistant

Harriet Bolwell
Front of House

Alex Brady
Box Office Supervisor/IT

Suzanne Brady
Box Office/
Drama Class Assistant

Neil Bratchpiece
Front of House

Laura Briggs
Front of House

Marion Brochard
Front of House

Louise Brown
Creative Learning
Officer

Andrew Bunton
Front of House

Lara Carter
Drama Class Assistant

Guy Coletta
Sound Technician/
Sound Designer

Lisa Corr
Drama Class Tutor

Natalia Cortes
Company Stage
Manager

Elaine G Coyle
Head of Wardrobe

Carol Cull
Housekeeper

Maureen Dalton
Front of House
Duty Manager

Lesley Davidson
Head of Operations

Denise Differ
Box Office Manager

Miriam Sarah Doren
Drama Class Assistant

Michael Dorrance
Deputy Head of
Workshop

Ann Dundas
Housekeeper

Lisa Dundas
Box Office

Paul Dundas
Box Office/
FOH Duty Manager

Julia Easton
Box Office

Sophie Fernie
Front of House

Fiona Findlater
Assistant Stage
Manager

Gillian Firth
Director of
Development

Barry Forde
Assistant Stage
Manager

Neil Francis
Drama Class Tutor

Jacky Gardiner
Front of House

Harvey Gardner
Front of House

Robert Gear
Carpenter

Vasso Georgiadou
Front of House

Anne Gillan
Finance Officer

Elly Goodman
Community Drama
Artist

Jamie Hayes
Head of Stage

Neil Haynes
Head Scenic Artist

Jill Henderson
Drama Class Assistant

Dominic Hill
Artistic Director

Guy Hollands
Associate Director
(Citizens Learning)

Stuart Jenkins
Head of Lighting
and Sound

Debbie Jones
Front of House

Jenny Howes
RSC Technical
Placement

Judith Kilvington
Executive Director

Jennifer Knotts
Front of House

Carmen Lam
Development Assistant

Campbell Lawrie
Box Office/
Drama Class Supervisor

Karen Lee
Wardrobe Assistant/
Dresser

Claire Lowney
Marketing Assistant

Robert MacFarlane
Wardrobe
Assistant/Cutter

Alison MacKinnon
Head of Marketing and
Communications

Lauren Macluskie
Front of House

Ruaridh Mathieson
Front of House

Carly McCaig
Creative Learning
Assistant

Erin McCardie
Front of House

THE LIBERTINE

Stephen Jeffreys

For Sue Edwards

Characters

JOHN WILMOT, *Second Earl of Rochester*
GEORGE ETHEREGE, *a playwright*
CHARLES SACKVILLE, *Earl of Dorset and Middlesex*
HARRY HARRIS, *an actor*
BILLY DOWNS, *a young spark*
JANE, *a prostitute*
MOLLY LUSCOMBE, *a stage manager*
MRS WILL UFTON, *a coffee-house proprietor*
TOM ALCOCK, *a servingman*
ELIZABETH BARRY, *an actress*
ELIZABETH MALET, *a country wife*
CHARLES II, *a monarch*

And PLAYGOERS, WHORES, CLIENTS, GUARDS, WATCH

Act One

Scene One   Will's Coffee House, 1675, morning
Scene Two   Dorset Gardens Theatre, the same day
Scene Three   St James's Park, the next morning
Scene Four   Dorset Gardens Theatre, that afternoon
Scene Five   Dog and Bitch Yard, that night
Scene Six   Rochester's London home, next day
Scene Seven   Whitehall Gardens, that night

Act Two

Scene Eight   Windsor Great Park, 1676
Scene Nine   Epsom, next day
Scene Ten   East End of London, a few weeks later
Scene Eleven   The Palace of Whitehall, that evening
Scene Twelve   Dorset Gardens Theatre, a few weeks later
Scene Thirteen   Adderbury, a few days later

The action moves continuously from scene to scene without any breaks except for the interval.

Author's Note

For dramatic reasons I have slightly compressed and rearranged events in Rochester's life without, I hope, distorting the historical record. In the original production the parts of Sackville and Harris were doubled: I would prefer these parts to be played by two different actors, but if this is not possible, lines ascribed to Sackville in scenes where Harris appears should be taken by Etherege or Downs.

S.J.

Prologue

Lights up. ROCHESTER *comes forward.*

ROCHESTER. Allow me to be frank at the commencement:
you will not like me. No, I say you will not. The gentlemen
will be envious and the ladies will be repelled. You will not
like me now and you will like me a good deal less as we go
on. Oh yes, I shall *do* things you will like. You will say 'That
was a noble impulse in him' or 'He played a brave part
there', but DO NOT WARM TO ME, it will not serve. When
I become a BIT OF A CHARMER that is your danger sign
for it prefaces the change into THE FULL REPTILE a few
seconds later. What I require is not your *affection* but your
attention. I must not be ignored or you will find me as
troublesome a package of humanity as ever pissed into the
Thames. Now. Ladies. An announcement. (*Looks around.*) I
am up for it. All the time. That's not a boast. Or an opinion.
It is bone-hard medical fact. I put it around, d'y'know? And
you will watch me putting it around and sigh for it. Don't. It
is a deal of trouble for you and you are better off watching
and drawing your conclusions from a distance than you
would be if I got my tarse pointing up your petticoats.
Gentlemen. (*Looks around.*) Do not despair, I am up for that
as well. When the mood is on me. And the same warning
applies. Now, gents: if there be vizards in the house, jades,
harlots (as how could there not be) leave them be for the
moment. Still your cheesy erections till I have had my say.
But later when you shag – and later you *will* shag, I shall
expect it of you and I will know if you have let me down – I
wish you to shag with my homuncular image rattling in your
gonads. Feel how it was for me, how it is for me and ponder.
'Was that shudder the same shudder he sensed? Did he know
something more profound? Or is there some wall of
wretchedness that we all batter with our heads at that

shining, livelong moment?' That is it. That is my prologue, nothing in rhyme, certainly no protestations of modesty, you were not expecting that, I trust. I reiterate only for those who have arrived late or were buying oranges or were simply not listening: I am John Wilmot, Second Earl of Rochester and I do not want you to like me.

ROCHESTER *goes. Lights come up on Scene One.*

Scene One – Coffee

WILL*'s coffee house.* ETHEREGE *and* SACKVILLE *sit over coffee at a long wooden table. Each has a pile of pages from a manuscript in front of him. It is a pirated copy of Dryden's latest play. They rustle and pick their way through it like scavengers. At another table,* JANE *sits staring into space.*

ETHEREGE. Any good bits yet?

SACKVILLE. Couldn't write a laundry list.

ETHEREGE. Good bits or bad bits, sound the alarm.

SACKVILLE. Couldn't write the menu at Lockett's.

ETHEREGE. Be fair, the menu at Lockett's isn't posted up in rhymed couplets.

SACKVILLE. And Dryden's supposed to be the Laureate.

ETHEREGE (*rummaging*). Good bits, bad bits.

SACKVILLE (*stopping*). I don't believe this.

ETHEREGE. Bad bit?

SACKVILLE. Tom's not really going to put this on, is he?

ETHEREGE. He put the last one on, what was it called?

SACKVILLE. *Amboyna*.

DOWNS, *a fresh-faced young man, comes in nervously.*

ETHEREGE. Billy!

SACKVILLE. *Amboyna*. A propagandist tragedy in blank verse.

ETHEREGE. Billy, join us. Coffee ho!

SACKVILLE. Put more people off fighting for their country than the invention of chain shot.

ETHEREGE. Billy Downs, this is Charles Sackville –

DOWNS (*overawed*). My lord, I am obliged to –

ETHEREGE. – Lord Buckhurst, Earl of Dorset.

SACKVILLE. And Middlesex.

ETHEREGE. And Middlesex –

SACKVILLE. You left out poxy Middlesex.

ETHEREGE. His Earlship is touchy this morning –

SACKVILLE. It's a big county.

ETHEREGE. We've got the original copy of Dryden's new play.

SACKVILLE. Friendly actor.

ETHEREGE. Here, have a wadge. Good bits and bad bits, that's
what we're after.

> ETHEREGE *doles out a helping of the play to* DOWNS,
> *then notices* JANE.

> (*To* JANE.) Madam. We are living through a golden age of
> the Arts and Sciences. Your grandchildren will want you to
> have partaken. You can't just sit there cleaning the gubbins
> out of your ears. Have some of this. (*Doles out pages*.) Act
> Four. Find a good bit, find a bad bit, give us a 'Hola'.

JANE. How do I tell the difference?

ETHEREGE. These days everyone's a critic. No training
required.

JANE. Can't read much.

ETHEREGE. Look at the shape. It tends to be bad when the
characters start conversing in ten-line slabs.

DOWNS. Doesn't Mr Dryden come in here sometimes?

ETHEREGE. That's the point. We find the good bits and the
bad bits, knock up a quick parody and have it circulating the
tables when he makes his entrance this afternoon.

MRS WILL UFTON *comes in with dishes of coffee*.

MRS WILL. Coffee, gents.

SACKVILLE. Excuse me, Mr Downs, but Dryden doesn't *come* in. He *slithers* in. Like a sewer man entering a blocked privy. Picks out a couple of young nearly dead poets, scrounges a drink and sprays dull praise and duller critique around in more or less equal doses, then slithers out again to cop a grudging toss off his whore. He is a squidgy, sanctimonious, shifting sort of gent, the Laureate. I'll wager any odds he'll turn Catholic in time for the next reign.

MRS WILL. He always puts his dish back on my tray when he has done with supping. I think that shows distinction.

ETHEREGE. To work, we've only got a couple of hours.

SACKVILLE. It ain't no caper without Johnny.

ETHEREGE. Charlie –

SACKVILLE. Don't Charlie me. It ain't no caper and you know it. I can make a stab at Dryden, you can make a stab at Dryden, but no one brings him off like Johnny.

ETHEREGE. Well, he's banished. Short of bowling down the Palace and begging the King on our benders to bring him back there's nothing we can do. So bear up.

SACKVILLE. It's *dull* without him. We didn't get Old Rowley back on the throne so he could make things dull.

ETHEREGE. Just keep rallying, good bits and bad bits.

MRS WILL (*to* JANE). You. Out.

JANE. I ain't doin' nuthink.

MRS WILL. I stand for a lot on these premises, but not jades touting for custom.

ETHEREGE. Leave her be, Mrs Will.

MRS WILL. She's taking up space.

ETHEREGE. I'll get her a coffee. Here's a penny.

DOWNS. What's this play called?

ETHEREGE. *Aureng-Zebe*.

DOWNS. *Aureng-Zebe*?

ETHEREGE. He's the hero. Play takes place in Agra, bit of exotica. Give all the characters funny names, set it in a place no one's ever been to and talking in blank verse don't seem so damned silly.

MRS WILL. Costumes come cheaper too. They get them towels out.

SACKVILLE. Bad bit, got a bad bit, got a very, very bad bit.

  ROCHESTER *comes in and stands at the back, watching.*

ETHEREGE. That's the spirit!

DOWNS. Let's have it, my lord.

ETHEREGE. Let the dog off the leash.

SACKVILLE. Stand by your posts, gents. This is Arimant, Governor of Agra. He's talking to Melesinda, wife of Morat:

  SACKVILLE *stands and declaims in the heroic manner.*

  'I come with haste surprising news to bring:
  In two hours' time since last I saw the king,
  The affairs of Court have wholly changed their face:
  Unhappy Aureng-Zebe is in disgrace;
  And your Morat, proclaimed the successor,
  Is called, to awe the city with his power.

  Those trumpets his triumphant entry tell,
  And now the shouts waft near the citadel.'

  The WITS *hoot and thump.*

  Now you have to admit, George –

ETHEREGE. I do, I do, that is an absolute –

DOWNS. It is a turd of a speech.

SACKVILLE. Some poor toss of an actor will have to soldier through that. Just doing it then, it feels *leaden*.

ETHEREGE. We got that, didn't we, Billy?

ROCHESTER. Gents, the speech is out of date:
    The affairs of Court have wholly changed their tack:
    Wronged Aureng-Zebe now is summoned back.

SACKVILLE. Johnny!

ETHEREGE. We were pining for you, even now we were
    pining!

The WITS *greet* ROCHESTER, *but he keeps his distance.*

ROCHESTER. Dryden. Dryden is the quarry, is he?

ETHEREGE. We have his new play. The idea is –

ROCHESTER. Good bits and bad bits. Quick parody. Everyone
    reading it when Dryden comes in this afternoon.

ETHEREGE. Are we so easy to fathom?

ROCHESTER. When I wake up in the country I dream of
    being in London. Then when I come to London I hate it.
    Except for Jane.

ETHEREGE. Put her down, this ain't Dog and Bitch Yard. We
    are after our bit of fun and Christ's wounds we need it when
    you're not here.

SACKVILLE. And we shall have it.

MRS WILL. I'll fetch coffee for you, my lord.

ROCHESTER. And one for my Jane too.

    MRS WILL *goes.*

SACKVILLE. Come on, John, tell us about Old Rowley, why
    did he bring you back?

DOWNS. Why did he banish you in the first place, my lord?

ROCHESTER. Who is this beardless youth who has been
    allowed out to hear my corrupting conversation?

ETHEREGE. This is Mr Downs, Mr Downs, the Earl of –

ROCHESTER. How old are you, Mr Downs?

ETHEREGE. Sixteen, my lord.

ROCHESTER. Young man, you will die of this company, no,
don't laugh I'm serious. But what does it matter if you die?
This is only conversation, you understand, it is not to be
confused with religion or philosophy, we talk like this because
we are *bored*, our boredom is so intense we make dangerous
things happen. (*Pause.*) Well, I have warned you and you have
not escaped so let the consequences be on your head.

ETHEREGE. Johnny?

ROCHESTER. This reign is a shambles, do you not think?
Coffee ho! My father risked life and limb hiding that *thing*
Charles up an oak tree, trudged by night WITH A HAWK
ON HIS WRIST – sophisticated notion of disguise my pater
had – TRUDGED through some particularly swampy bits of
England on a third-rate horse in the company of *tedious*
people and *to what purpose*?

ETHEREGE. He's forgiven you –

ROCHESTER. He's forgiven me, I can't forgive him.

SACKVILLE. So why did he banish you?

MRS WILL *comes in with coffee for* ROCHESTER.

ROCHESTER. Thank you, Mrs Will. So why did he banish me?
Well, it is a fine morning I am walking through the galleries,
the King is walking through the galleries, I am splendidly
alone, he is surrounded by a slow-moving troupe of
Mediterranean dignitaries –

SACKVILLE. The wife's family –

ROCHESTER. And he *must* make a show of me. Behold the
Earl of Rochester, the Gent, the Wit, the Poet! Pray let us
have some of your muse now. What am I to do? I must not
extemporise for it always turns out so bawdy. Then I recall,
in my pocket I have a sketch of something rustic with
nymphs, I pull it out – (*Pulling out paper.*) and deliver:

'I' th' isle of Britain, long since famous grown
For breeding th' best cunts in Christendom – '

'Rat me', thinks I, 'this is not the piece of paper I had
supposed.' The sovereign's eyes are more piercingly black
than I can remember, the jaws of his entourage are decidedly
earthbound, but I KNOW I DO NOT HAVE IT IN ME TO
STOP. The King knows I do not have it in me to stop.

ETHEREGE. Oh, Johnny.

ROCHESTER. IT GETS WORSE. This piece of paper is not
covered merely with the thump and slop of congress, no, no,
this poem is an attack on the monarchy itself, culminating in
a depiction of the Royal Mistress striving to flog the flaccid
Royal Member into a state of excitement:

'This you'd believe, had I but time to tell ye
The pains it costs to poor laborious Nelly,
Whilst she employs hands, fingers, mouth and thighs,
Ere she can raise the member she enjoys.
All monarchs I hate, and the thrones they sit on,
From the hector of France to the cully of Britain.'

A ghastly silence. MRS WILL, *distraught, goes back to her
kitchen. The* WITS *and* JANE *begin to giggle.*

ETHEREGE. It is damn'd good though, Johnny.

ROCHESTER. Of course it's good, that's not the point. The
point is, *he* couldn't appreciate it. The eye freezes me, he
tosses his periwig and sweeps on with the wife's family in
tow. Took me a couple of hours to write that poem – JUST
TO PLEASE HIM – not only didn't raise a laugh, two
months in the country at the height of the season, missed all
the good plays.

ETHEREGE. Come on, Johnny, cheer yourself up, give us an
improvised stanza on our whole company and we'll laugh in
the King's place.

SACKVILLE. Yes, boring Old Rowley, we love you, Johnny,
let's have more stanzas!

ROCHESTER. Stanzas on the company? What good fortune we are not four and twenty. Where shall I start?

SACKVILLE. With me.

ROCHESTER. Well, that's easy:

Charles Sackville
Was the first to swyve
The young Nell Gwyn it's reckoned:
So though our King
Has since shagged Gwyn
He's only Charles the second.

The WITS *thump the table in appreciation.*

SACKVILLE. Damn you, Johnny, now you've made me melancholy for my sonsie Nell.

ROCHESTER. Well, she ain't your sonsie Nell any more, Chas, and the sooner you get used to it, the sooner your pecker will rise again to useful service.

ETHEREGE. Me, me.

ROCHESTER. Ah, Gentle George, what more can be said of him?

To Etherege
I drink a pledge
His life has run the gamut:
He's penned naught good
Since *She Would If She Could*
He would if he could but he cannot.

The WITS *hammer the table again.*

ETHEREGE. Well, Johnny, it was a damned well-said thing, but it ain't true, d'y'see.

ROCHESTER. Oh, but it is true, Georgie. You're one of those literary types who think they can enjoy the town's esteem for ever for something they wrote seven years ago. You can't be promising for ever. Sooner or later you have to *do* something.

ETHEREGE. That's what I'm saying. I've done it. I've written a new play.

A sensation. Everyone awaits ROCHESTER'*s reaction.*

ROCHESTER. Oooooh. Written a new play, has he? All those afternoons he was pretending to slope off and roger his mistress like a decent chap, he was lurking in his rooms poking away at a *play.*

SACKVILLE. That's disgusting, George.

ROCHESTER. Disgusting and shameful.

SACKVILLE. Come on, out with it. Tell us what it's called.

ETHEREGE. Well, it doesn't actually have a title yet.

SACKVILLE. No title.

ETHEREGE. It hasn't got a title or a fifth act.

ROCHESTER. Will you mark the poverty of the rogue's understanding? He lacks the two things which will ensure success –

SACKVILLE. The title to draw the crowd in –

ROCHESTER. – and the fifth act to send them away content.

DOWNS. A man may fill the gap between these two mighty abstractions with any dross.

ETHEREGE. What I do have is a central character –

ROCHESTER. What's he called?

ETHEREGE. Dorimant.

ROCHESTER. Dorimant, Christ's wounds that's subtle. Don't tell me it's based on Dryden.

ETHEREGE. Pox o' Dryden, it's based on *you.*

Pause. The moment is dangerous.

ROCHESTER. And do you tell the truth about me?

ETHEREGE. I… I have attempted to show you as –

ROCHESTER. Yes?

ETHEREGE. Well, I enjoy your company, my lord, and I –

ROCHESTER. You've made me endearing, haven't you?

ETHEREGE. Only the public can judge –

ROCHESTER. Don't smarm around, you've made me endearing.

ETHEREGE. You're an endearing sort of chap –

ROCHESTER. So you haven't told the truth. (*Pause*.) Good. Don't want to go frightening people. We are the merry wits after all, ain't we? We are the froth and fizz of the reign. Once people tumble to the fact that *we're* not happy they'll start to question the purpose of the whole enterprise, won't they? So, endearing. Well done, George, I drink to you. But only in coffee.

ROCHESTER *drinks*.

ALCOCK *sprawls on, propelled by* MRS WILL.

MRS WILL. Get your filching carcass out my shop!

ROCHESTER. Mrs Will, on what account are you behaving so forcefully towards this drudge?

MRS WILL. On account of his dishonesty.

ROCHESTER. Dishonesty?

MRS WILL. While my back was turned, this fellow helps himself to two shillings that I had set aside with a mind to paying the milkman who always calls on a Tuesday.

ROCHESTER. A thief and a rogue.

MRS WILL. My lord, you express it.

ROCHESTER. Haven't quite got the hang of the reign, have you, Mrs Will? Perhaps you've not noticed, but since our sovereign rogerer supreme returned from France, what is it fifteen years ago, your brand of puritanical nit-picking has been in decline.

MRS WILL. It is a dishonest rogue –

ROCHESTER. Your adherence to these outmoded codes of behaviour is quaint and touching –

MRS WILL. I will not employ a thief –

ROCHESTER. Then I will. (*To* ALCOCK.) On your feet.

ALCOCK *stands*. ROCHESTER *reaches into his purse*.

How much was Mrs Will paying you?

ALCOCK. Eight shillings a week, sir.

ROCHESTER. Who talks of thieving? Here's five pound in gold. Go to my man outside, his name is Roland, you will know him from his dismal manner and sluice-gate nostrils. Deliver this money into his hand, tell him I am dispensing with his services and that you, being appointed in his stead, should have his livery in exchange for your own rags. Go, see it is done.

ALCOCK *goes with the money*.

MRS WILL. He will run off with the gold and that will be your lesson.

ROCHESTER. I do hope so. If he turn honest after coming within my orbit, I am not the malicious planet I had hoped. Mr Downs, reveal yourself, do you think I dispense wisely in this matter?

DOWNS. If the rogue... if the rogue run off with the gold, well, then you have proved a point... but at your own loss... if he return in your livery... well, you have gained a servant who is a proven cheat. So you prove a different point but again at your own expense.

ROCHESTER. You summarise well, Mr Downs, and in such a manner I deduce you were trained at one of the count-the-angels-on-a-pinhead Cambridge colleges, King's, was it not?

DOWNS. It was, my lord –

ROCHESTER. King's yes, and yet, or possibly and so, you do not draw the general moral of the incident, which is?

DOWNS. Which is…

ROCHESTER. Which is that any experiment of interest in life will be carried out at your own expense. Mark it well.

ALCOCK *comes back in a footman's livery.*

What? You are returned?

ALCOCK. I am, sir.

ROCHESTER. And where's the money?

ALCOCK. I gave it to your fellow and cashiered him.

ROCHESTER. Then you are turned honest, I cannot support that.

ALCOCK. I regret the deed's honesty, my lord, but I considered that if I performed it and fell into your service, I would have more enjoyment of life.

SACKVILLE. More enjoyment of life!

ROCHESTER. See, this fellow has the hang of the reign. I like this fellow exceedingly. What is your name?

ALCOCK. Alcock, my lord.

ROCHESTER. Better and better!

ETHEREGE. Like master, like servant.

SACKVILLE. Alcock, in his livery you stand proud.

ROCHESTER. You shall drink and shag more than any servingman in the kingdom.

ALCOCK. How shall I begin, my lord?

ROCHESTER. Go at once and spend this money on a whore – no, not Jane – I wish her to be large and greasy – then, when you are done, return here.

ALCOCK. My lord –

ROCHESTER. Be gone!

ALCOCK *goes.*

ETHEREGE. Perhaps I'm getting on, but it does seem a trifle early for that particular indulgence.

ROCHESTER. He will never be my servant if he don't understand excess.

JANE (*perking up*). Found a good bit.

SACKVILLE. What?

JANE. Them papers you give me. Found a good bit.

ROCHESTER. How do you know?

JANE. Smell. He done this bit before he had his dinner. See, next bit's got a gravy stain. When men do a good bit they reward themselves straight away.

ROCHESTER (*taking papers*). See, gents, an admirable critic! Let's put you to the test and see what Mr Dryden was inspired to pen before his chop and gravy:

'When I consider life 'tis all a cheat;
Yet, fooled with hope, men favour the deceit;'

ETHEREGE. Oh profound!

ROCHESTER. 'Tum-ti-tum repay: da-de-da-former day:
Lies worse... blest, new joys... possest,
Strange cozenage! None would live past years again,
Yet all hope pleasure in what yet remain;
And, from the dregs of life, think to receive,
What the first sprightly running could not give.
I'm tired of waiting for this chemic gold,
Which fools us young, and beggars us when old.'

JANE. There you are, gents, good bit. Told you. Good day.

ROCHESTER. Jane! Where shall I find you?

JANE. The Playhouse. The yard. London's small.

JANE *goes*.

SACKVILLE. The bastard. He wrote a good bit.

ETHEREGE. He wrote a classic bit.

SACKVILLE. How can he do this to me? Just when you think he's written out.

ROCHESTER. 'And, from the dregs of life, think to receive,
What the first sprightly running could not give.
I'm tired of waiting for this chemic gold,
Which fools us young, and beggars us when old.'

Well, gents, you came to mock the Laureate and he marched
away with the bays. It would sober a man, would it not, if a
man could but remember how it was to be sober.

ETHEREGE. Bear up, Johnny. Racing at Epsom tomorrow.

ROCHESTER. Tomorrow, my wife and I are invited for Pall-
Mall in St James Park tomorrow.

SACKVILLE. Your wife?

ETHEREGE. You brought your wife to London?

ROCHESTER. We are to sit for our portrait, an immortality
which I would dearly avoid, but my mother demands it. But
for now, gents, I long to see Otway's new play this
afternoon.

SACKVILLE. Then we shall go.

ETHEREGE. Otway. I do find it invigorating, all these new
young men coming into the theatre.

ROCHESTER. I have high hopes of Tom Otway. Mr Downs,
will you come with us?

DOWNS. I will, my lord, I love well a play.

ROCHESTER. Downs, you have a dying countenance, but
that's no matter. First to the inn and then the Playhouse!

ALL. The Playhouse!!

They sweep off.

Scene Two – Playhouse

Immediately a spotlight picks out ELIZABETH BARRY, *dressing in the tiring house for the role of Draxilla in* Alcibiades. *She is in her teens, dark with strong features. She talks to the audience.*

BARRY. The part of Draxilla in Otway's *Alcibiades* is what is commonly called thankless. You are the second female which means you are courted late in the play and shoved out of the way early. The most important thing to remember is that the level of your passion must never rival that of Mrs Betterton who is – in the play – your best friend. If Mrs Betterton's soul is in torment, then Elizabeth Barry's must only be in mild distress. I do not complain, it is a living. But it is the kind of role where your fellow actors become uncommonly generous with advice culled from their years of experience on the stage.

HARRIS *comes on, a youngish actor on the make.*

HARRIS. Mrs Barry. Lizzie. There is an area of the play in which I feel I am able to help you.

BARRY. That is very generous of you, Mr Harris.

HARRIS. There is a lapse you are falling into – a very common lapse, one which I suffered from in my own first roles, and the correction of which was effected by a more senior member of the company to whom I was eternally grateful.

BARRY. What do you wish me to do?

HARRIS. Act Three, Scene Three, at the camp.

BARRY. Patroclus and Draxilla, yes?

HARRIS. Where I protest my love. Let us essay the passage beginning 'Lovers whose flights – '

BARRY *picks up the passage immediately.*

BARRY. 'Lovers whose flights so sublime pitches choose,
Oft soar too high, and so their quarry loose.
But you Sir know to moderate your height,
Missing your game can eas'ly slack the flight.'

HARRIS. 'Such faint essays may fit a common flame,
  But my desires have a far nobler Aime,
  Religious honour, and a zeal that's true,
  Rais'd by that Deity to which I sue.'

BARRY. 'Those who to deities their offerings pay,
  Make their addresses in an humbler way.
  Not in confidence of what they give,
  But modest hopes of what they shall receive – '

HARRIS. There, you see, Mrs Barry. You must show the *idea* of
  modest hopes.

BARRY. Except that the modest hopes are not mine, they would
  be yours.

HARRIS. It makes no difference. The modest hopes of the
  devout supplicant are what *possesses* the audience at this
  moment.

BARRY. But I am seeking to deter your love, am I not? Should
  I not show 'em that?

HARRIS. No, Lizzie, you should not. Modest hopes, show me
  modest hopes. Again.

  BARRY *follows* HARRIS'*s instructions.*

BARRY 'Those who to deities their offerings pay,
  Make their addresses in an humbler way.
  Not in confidence of what they give,
  But modest hopes of what they shall receive – '

HARRIS. Good, Lizzie, good. Modest hopes, modest hopes.
  Paint 'em a picture of what you're saying.

BARRY. Thank you, Mr Harris.

  LUSCOMBE, *the stage manager, bustles by with her
  loud voice.*

LUSCOMBE. To your places, please, Mr Harris, I do hope you
  will favour us with the prologue in its entirety today and not
  merely the bits that happen to catch your fancy. All Act One
  beginners to your places, Mrs Barry, that is a dress you are

wearing, not a collection of dusters. Ten seconds to curtain up. The curtain is UP!!!

We go front of house. HARRIS *comes onstage.*
ROCHESTER, ETHEREGE *and* DOWNS *are together in a box. On the other side of the stage are the* PIT ROWDIES – KEDGEO, ALCOCK *and a* VIZARD. JANE *stands with the* PIT, *holding a basket of oranges. The* AUDIENCE *frequently overlap the* ACTORS, *especially* HARRIS.

JANE. Half past two in the afternoon. Hot, itchy. Three hundred partially washed people. We are not here to see a play. We are here to meet, gawp, flaunt, chatter, filch, ogle, buy and sell against a general background of blank verse.

HARRIS. 'To you known judges of what's sence and wit,
Our Authour swears he gladly will submit.
But there's a sort of things infest the Pit,
That will be witty spite of Nature too,'

DOWNS. Have a care, sir!

ALCOCK. Oi, you! Gissanorange!

JANE. Three for sevenpence.

ALCOCK. I don't want three I want one.

HARRIS. 'And to be thought so, haunt and pester you.
Hither sometimes those would be Witts repair,
In quest of you; where if you not appear,
Crys one – Pugh! Damn me what do we do here?'

ALCOCK. Kedgeo! Is Colin coming?

KEDGEO. I dunno, do I?

ALCOCK (*to* JANE). Give us two.

JANE. Thass sixpence.

VIZARD. Kedgeo, that your name?

KEDGEO. Thass Colin there.

ALCOCK. Colin!

VIZARD. You won't never find a tighter one than mine.

HARRIS. 'Strait up he starts, his Garniture then puts
    In order, so he Cocks and out he struts.'

VIZARD. Or I'll frig you right now, soft hands but firm.

KEDGEO (*to* VIZARD). Do leave off.

ALCOCK (*throwing an orange to* KEDGEO). Here, Kedge,
    juice your squeaker!

KEDGEO. Gent, Tom!

DOWNS. This prologue is fine, do you not think, Mr Etherege.

ETHEREGE. Any dolt can write a prologue.

DOWNS. Though to my taste the prologues in Paris are finer.

HARRIS. 'Wit has indeed a stranger been of late,
    'Mongst its pretenders nought so strange as that.
    Both Houses too so long a Fast have known,
    That courest Non-sence goes most glibly down.'

VIZARD. Mr Etherege! Take a nibble?

ETHEREGE. Had my dinner, thank you, madam.

DOWNS. Oh ha, George!

HARRIS. 'Thus though this Trifler never wrote before,
    Yet Faith he ventur'd on the common score:
    Since Non-sence is so generally allowed,
    He hopes that this may pass among the Crowd.'

    Applause for HARRIS. *A little barracking.*

JANE. It was a quiet afternoon till Mrs Barry appeared. It was
    not just that she was bad, though she was worse than
    anything I had ever seen, but there was a superior manner to
    her badness that could not be borne.

BARRY. 'The serving you, my happiness secures,
    I'm only somthing by my being yours;
    Since equally with yours, my hopes were crost,
    When in your Lover I a Brother lost;'

JANE. The Pit went for her like a dog to a raw throat.

KEDGEO. Dog!

VIZARD. Bitch!!

ALCOCK. Dragon!!!

JANE. She stood and took it, but then, had she scuttled off there
   would have been no wages. The office clerks in the cheaper
   boxes joined in the rallying, then the middle and top galleries.

   All but ROCHESTER *hoot and jeer. Suddenly the sound cuts
   out and we see* BARRY *through his eyes.*

BARRY. 'Then like an Orphan destitute and bare
   Of all but misery and sad despair,
   Your Kindness gave my yeelding spirits rest,
   And rais'd me to a dwelling in your breast:
   Then ought I not in all my soul resign,
   To ease her griefs that kindly pitty'd mine?'

ROCHESTER. 'Then ought I not in all my soul resign…'

   The AUDIENCE *chant 'Off! Off! Off!'*

JANE. I almost felt sorry for the stuck-up bitch.

   The tiring house. BARRY *comes, sits down, and looks at
   herself in the mirror. She wipes angrily at her face.*
   LUSCOMBE *comes in, holding a note.*

BARRY. Yes, I know!

LUSCOMBE. No, you do not know.

BARRY. I know!

LUSCOMBE. Well, if you know, why do you persist in doing
   the opposite?

BARRY. Because –

LUSCOMBE. Because you are a sort I have met before. You
   are a sort who thinks they are above it. Well, they are not
   above it, what they are above is themselves. If girls like you
   do not do what they're told, it is all up with our sex on the

stage. You cannot ignore the advice of them that know. Them that know know because them that went before told them. And if them that come after don't heed, then there will be others that will and here is a note from Mr Betterton which I suspect says as much.

LUSCOMBE *gives her the note. She does not open it right away.* HARRIS *comes in, towelling himself.*

Teach her something, Mr Harris, she will take nothing from me.

HARRIS. Lizzie, the work we did beforehead –

LUSCOMBE. Tell her –

HARRIS. Did it mean nothing to you?

BARRY. That is correct, Mr Harris.

ETHEREGE *and* DOWNS *come in. They have come backstage to ogle the actresses.*

HARRIS. Molly, I cannot teach those who are not disposed to learn. Mr Etherege, how do you do, sir?

BARRY *opens the note, reads it, crumples it.*

ETHEREGE. Well, Mr Harris, well.

HARRIS. Did you not care for the play?

ETHEREGE. Oh, the play, the play was well enough.

DOWNS. And most of the acting too was fine, Mr Harris –

SACKVILLE. You wear that tunic damn well.

DOWNS. Your prologue, very fine indeed.

ALCOCK *comes in. He bears a bunch of flowers.*

ALCOCK. Where is Mrs Barry?

LUSCOMBE. Who wants her?

ALCOCK (*spotting* BARRY). I bring these for you, Mrs Barry. From a gentleman.

BARRY. What gentleman?

ALCOCK. The Earl of Rochester.

ETHEREGE. Alcock, where is your master?

ALCOCK. Having discourse with Mr Betterton, sir.

At once ROCHESTER *sweeps in.*

ROCHESTER. Molly. Ah. Mrs Barry.

LUSCOMBE. On your feet, Lizzie.

BARRY *stands and curtsies, the ordeal unending.*

ROCHESTER. You have received my gift?

BARRY. I have, my lord. But not its meaning.

ROCHESTER. I bring communication from Mr Betterton.

ROCHESTER *hands her a note.*

BARRY. I have had such already.

LUSCOMBE (*to* ETHEREGE). She has been dismissed.

ROCHESTER. This is quite another.

BARRY *reads the note. She looks at* ROCHESTER.

BARRY. You have obtained a reprieve for me.

ROCHESTER. Yes, madam, but there is a price.

BARRY. What price?

ROCHESTER. This is your first season on the London stage?

BARRY. It is, my lord.

ROCHESTER. And the work is pleasing to you?

BARRY. My lord, why do you make me an object of your fun? I do not please the house and you know it. They goad me worse each day.

ROCHESTER. What is the use in pleasing apes? You pleased *me*. What need have you of pleasing others? Speak me that speech again.

BARRY. What speech?

ROCHESTER. 'The serving you.' I would hear it again, now.
That is the price of your reprieve.

BARRY *settles herself and plays the speech.*

BARRY. 'The serving you, my happiness secures,
I'm only somthing by my being yours;
Since equally with yours, my hopes were crost,
When in your Lover I a Brother lost;
Then like an Orphan destitute and bare
Of all but misery and sad despair,
Your Kindness gave my yeelding spirits rest,
And rais'd me to a dwelling in your breast:
Then ought I not in all my soul resign,
To ease her griefs that kindly pitty'd mine?'

ROCHESTER. You perform that speech with such a sense
of truth.

BARRY. Thank you, sir.

ROCHESTER. But I would have conversation with you.

BARRY. Yes, my lord.

ROCHESTER. I mean on the subject of your acting. I have
much to impart to you.

BARRY. I shall be thankful for it.

ROCHESTER. First of all, Mrs Barry, you must acquire the trick
of ignoring those who do not like you. In my experience, those
who do not *like* you fall into two categories: the stupid, and
the envious. The stupid will like you in five years' time, the
envious never. You are already the most fascinating actress on
the London stage. With my training you will become the best.
I shall come to the theatre tomorrow.

BARRY. Come as you wish, I am always here.

BARRY *goes.* LUSCOMBE *follows.*

ETHEREGE. What are you up to, Johnny? She can't act.

DOWNS. She has neither the cadence of the heroic nor the posture.

ROCHESTER. Oh, you beat your critical clappers on the bell of your self-importance, do you, gentlemen?

ETHEREGE. She does everything too early or too late, sometimes both at once.

ROCHESTER. I will wager you a hundred guineas she will become the finest actress on our stage.

ETHEREGE. This is the prick talking, not the head, knob her and have done.

ROCHESTER. Is it a wager?

ETHEREGE. My dear friend, you do not have a hundred guineas.

ROCHESTER. Is it a wager?

ETHEREGE *extends his hand*.

HARRIS. *He* does not have to share a stage with her.

HARRIS *flounces out*.

ETHEREGE. Well, Billy, there ain't much to be had here.

DOWNS. Let's tope a quart at Oxford Kate's and sniff the traffic.

ETHEREGE. Tope's the word. Johnny, we'll keep a glass for you.

ETHEREGE *and* DOWNS *go*.

ROCHESTER. Alcock.

ALCOCK. My lord.

ROCHESTER. Something rotten has got into my guts.

ALCOCK. I trust it is not me, my lord.

ROCHESTER. No, Alcock, it is not.

ROCHESTER *goes. Lights fade quickly around* ALCOCK.

Scene Three – Pall-Mall

ALCOCK. The name of the game Pall-Mall is derived from two Italian words: *palla* meaning ball and *maglio* meaning mallet. See, I may look like a bit of an arsehole but I graze on scraps of erudition and regurgitate them at surprising moments. It's a marvellous recreation for the mornings, Pall-Mall, tip-top. In fact, it's the poxiest game ever invented. What's wrong is that the mood of repressed violence which hangs over the game is taken out on the balls, not on the players. But it keeps the nobs out in the air long enough to raise an appetite for the dinner that will be plonked in front of them an hour later.

ELIZABETH MALET *comes on.* ALCOCK *bows and hands her a mallet.*

Uno maglio, signora.

MALET. Alcock. That is your name, is it not?

ALCOCK. It is, my lady.

MALET. Have you seen my husband?

ALCOCK. He is drinking, madam, with Mr Etherege and young Mr Downs.

MALET. I am unused to my husband's London habits. Is it not too early to be drinking?

ALCOCK. No, madam. In my short employment with his lordship I have already observed that when it comes to drinking it is never too early and never too late.

MALET. In the country...

ALCOCK. Yes, my lady?

MALET. In the country he behaves differently.

Immediately, ROCHESTER, ETHEREGE, DOWNS *and* JANE *arrive on one side of the stage, while* KING CHARLES *and* SACKVILLE *arrive on the other.*

ALCOCK. The King!!

ROCHESTER *and* CHARLES *now indulge in a passage which is staged for the* ONLOOKERS – *a kind of press conference to show that* ROCHESTER *is back in favour.*

CHARLES. My Lord Rochester. I believe the English are the most intractable people upon earth.

ROCHESTER. I most humbly beg Your Majesty's pardon if I presume in that respect –

CHARLES. You would find them so were you in my place and obliged to govern.

ROCHESTER. In Your Majesty's place I would not govern at all.

CHARLES. How then?

ROCHESTER. I would send for my good Lord Rochester and command him to govern.

CHARLES. But the singular modesty of that nobleman!

ROCHESTER. He would certainly conform himself to Your Majesty's bright example! How gloriously would the two grand social virtues flourish under his auspices!

CHARLES. Oh, *prisca fides*! What can these be?

ROCHESTER. The love of wine and women.

CHARLES. God bless Your Majesty!

ROCHESTER. These attachments keep the world in good humour, and therefore I say they are social virtues. Let the Bishop of Salisbury deny it if he can –

CHARLES. He died last night; have you a mind to succeed him?

ROCHESTER. On condition that I shall never be called upon to preach on the thirtieth of January nor on the twenty-ninth of May.

CHARLES. These conditions are curious. You object to the first, it being the anniversary of my father's martyrdom and therefore a melancholy subject, but the other is the anniversary of my Restoration –

ROCHESTER. And therefore a melancholy subject too.

A pause. ROCHESTER *has gone too far.*

CHARLES. That is too much –

ROCHESTER. Nay, I only mean that a sermon would be a little too grave for the day. Nothing but the indulgence of the two grand social virtues could be a proper testimony of my joy upon that occasion.

CHARLES. Thou art the happiest fellow in my dominions! Let me perish if I do not envy thee thy impudence.

ROCHESTER *bows. The* ONLOOKERS, *relieved, applaud.*

Lord Buckhurst. Pick the teams. By your rank, you must be the other captain. I will have her – (*Points to* JANE.) on my side.

SACKVILLE *organises teams. They toss up, commence play and follow the first hits off the stage.* CHARLES *takes* ROCHESTER *aside to speak privately.*

The verbal gymnastics are still up to snuff.

ROCHESTER. A bottle of claret either side of breakfast is ever a spur to a man's wit.

CHARLES. I'd like to explain something, Johnny. When you first came to Court, you were a boy of eighteen and I was only five years into the reign. A certain flippancy, a little whiff of impertinence, this was acceptable. But we're ten years further down the road and the view is different, d'y'see?

ROCHESTER. You're not going to offer me a job, are you?

CHARLES. No, I'm not.

ROCHESTER. Ambassador to the English crown in Lyons.

CHARLES. I could have ignored your pornographic poem but I made a fuss about it for a specific reason. The tone has to change. The way the reign appears. I've got another fight coming up with those Parliament bastards. Money. You know I can't keep the country going on what they give me, but I don't want to lock antlers with them head-on the way my father did.

ROCHESTER. Head-on, that's quite a good –

CHARLES. I have to look responsible, sober. I want you with me. I want you to take a new role.

ROCHESTER. At the Playhouse?

CHARLES. No, the House of Lords. Between our families there have always been duties and rewards. Your father spirited me out of England when my life was at stake. So I looked after him and after you.

ROCHESTER. You put me in the Tower –

CHARLES. And I let you out.

The PLAYERS *cross the stage.*

The time has come to pay your dues. You can scribble your lampoons, you can shag your whores but keep it in the background. People listen to you. I want you on my side. Anyone can oppose, it's fun to be *against* things, but there comes a time when you have to start being *for* things as well.

ROCHESTER. What do you want?

CHARLES. I want a poem, a play, something of substance. You're better than all of them, Dryden, Sedley, the whole gang. I'll give you five hundred guineas and you will give me a major work of literature, something profound that will stand as a monument to my reign.

ROCHESTER. When would you like it, Friday?

CHARLES. Don't fuck it up, John, I love you.

CHARLES *joins the game.* ROCHESTER *stands alone,* MALET *runs on, holding a mallet.*

MALET. We should mark the front lawn at Adderbury for Pall-Mall. I had always thought it a foolish game.

ROCHESTER. Depends who you play it with.

MALET. But is it not irregular? That the King plays with a common prostitute but not his wife.

ROCHESTER. The Portuguese have little flair for outdoor pursuits. Except navigating, of course.

MALET. I mean that the etiquette of it is singular.

ROCHESTER. I KNOW WHAT YOU MEAN!

Pause.

MALET. You must always be Ace, King and Jack, my dear. But Heaven has not dispos'd your cards so. You are not happy when I am with you in London.

ROCHESTER. I am happier than I know. But the circumstances of this visit –

MALET. The Playhouse. Something passed at the Playhouse.

ROCHESTER. The Playhouse made me melancholy.

MALET. Why?

ROCHESTER. Because I do not take the pleasure in it I once did.

MALET. Your eyes shone on your return.

ROCHESTER. Only because I had seen my friends.

MALET. Well then. You must make the pleasures you have do and not be yearning for pleasures that are past.

ROCHESTER. I hate the thought that any pleasure may be past.

MALET. It is not for you to love or hate, but for you to know and accept. The loves of eight and twenty cannot compare with the loves of seventeen. You must love what is near to hand and not hanker after what is distant.

ROCHESTER. Yes. Yes, I must.

A moment. Then a shout from the PLAYERS.

ETHEREGE. My Lord Rochester. It is your shot, you know.

ROCHESTER. I'm not playing, George.

CHARLES. Oh, but you are, John. You are if I say.

MALET hands the mallet to ROCHESTER. *He goes off to play. Lighting narrows around her.*

MALET. He had gathered a party of armed men at Charing Cross to ambush me. I was eighteen and worth two and a half thousand pound a year. His underlings bundled me from my own coach and six into another and rattled me away on the road to Uxbridge. 'We take you to my Lord of Rochester,' one of them said and at once I was filled with a warm content. This was not a rape or a bid to abduct me for my fortune. It was a personal message. Of all the rich young lords who sniffed at my hand and my estate, he was the only one who thought to circumvent my guardians and address me in person. And so I dug in my heels and would not marry the others but held out for the one who had written me such a hot-headed note and been committed to the Tower for it. I married my lord because he was a romantic.

Lights fade to blackout.

Scene Four – Training Barry

Dorset Gardens Theatre, late morning. ROCHESTER *is led onto the stage by* LUSCOMBE, *jangling her keys.*

BARRY *is there.*

LUSCOMBE. I can't let you have long on stage, I must see to the preparation of *Tamburlaine* for this afternoon. I do not take much to *Tamburlaine*. It is a deal of setting up, three hours of rant and kettledrums and then a deal of taking down. I shall not dip my beak in my dinnerbowl till past eight o'clock.

LUSCOMBE *goes.* BARRY *and* ROCHESTER *stand on either side of the stage, a big distance between them.*

ROCHESTER. Mrs Barry.

BARRY. My Lord Rochester.

ROCHESTER. I am come, as I said I would.

BARRY. I thank you for speaking to Mr Betterton yesterday.

ROCHESTER. I am a patron of this theatre, it was my duty.

BARRY. No, my lord, I am indebted to you. (*Pause.*) Are you not sad to be returned to London? The country must be very fine now it is the spring.

ROCHESTER. It has many irritations as well. Now, Lizzie, I come to further your training and I would make a start.

BARRY. Will you have me lift my skirt or do you have a mind to raise it by your own endeavours?

ROCHESTER. I am come to train you in your acting.

BARRY. So you said when first we met. Your reputation being what it is, I thought you meant something else.

ROCHESTER. I have, I hope, many reputations. I am come, I say, to train you.

BARRY. Well, I am indebted to you, sir, but I never in my life heard you spoken of as an actor.

ROCHESTER. That does not deter me from spreading my insights to others.

BARRY. I thought it would not.

ROCHESTER. Then we shall begin?

BARRY. It seems we shall.

ROCHESTER. You are familiar with the plays of Mr Etherege?

BARRY. There are but two, my lord.

ROCHESTER. Not for long, I fear. *The Comical Revenge; or, Love in a Tub.* You have seen Mrs Betterton playing Graciana?

BARRY. Yes, I am her understudy.

ROCHESTER. And… you have an opinion of her performance?

BARRY. Mrs Betterton has a very pleasant speaking voice.

ROCHESTER. Indeed. Act Two, Scene Two. I shall play Beaufort.

Conversationally, ROCHESTER *slips into the scene, so that we barely notice the change.* BARRY, *however, immediately hits a more declamatory register and a tone of sweet innocence.*

'Graciana, why do you condemn your love?
Your beauty without that, alas! would prove
But my destruction, an unlucky star
Prognosticating ruin and despair.'

BARRY. 'Sir, you mistake; 'tis not my love I blame,
But my discretion: here the active flame
Should yet a longer time have been concealed;
Too soon, too soon I fear it was revealed.
Our weaker sex glories in surprise,
We boast the sudden conquests of our eyes:
But men esteem a foe that dares contend,
One that with noble courage does defend
A wounded heart; the victories men gain
They prize by their own hazard and their pain.'

ROCHESTER *stares at* BARRY.

ROCHESTER. That wasn't Elizabeth Barry, it was Mrs Betterton.

BARRY. An understudy must imitate, not create.

ROCHESTER. Yesterday you created.

BARRY. Yesterday I was dismissed.

ROCHESTER. But you played truthfully.

BARRY. It costs too much to play the truth.

ROCHESTER. I do not think you have considered this speech at all.

BARRY. I carry thirty-four parts in my head, the task is learning, not considering.

ROCHESTER. Well, let us consider now. What does it mean, that speech which Mrs Betterton mangles so?

BARRY. Graciana's meaning is… she means she has given away the secrets of her heart too freely. A thing that a gentlewoman must not do to a gentleman.

ROCHESTER. Why not?

BARRY. Because men will take love for granted and then not prize it.

ROCHESTER. And is our author right? Do you believe that?

BARRY. I believe men are hurdles that must be negotiated.

ROCHESTER. Is that all? Do you never feel passion for us?

BARRY. I have counterfeited passion in several beds if that is your meaning.

ROCHESTER. Counterfeit will not serve you on the stage.

BARRY. Yesterday I was jeered and taunted by four hundred ruffians. I know that will not serve me.

ROCHESTER. And so you'll take their word against both of ours and traffic in falsehood from now on.

BARRY. I don't know!

ROCHESTER. Then let us gain knowledge. To the speech again. You played it sweetly. Graciana is not innocent or she would not have such insight. If you had ever loved a man you would say that speech with regret, because you would fear the loss of him.

BARRY. Supposing I have loved and not told you.

ROCHESTER. Then show me in the speech. (*Cueing her.*) 'Prognosticating ruin and despair.'

BARRY *is within an ace of walking away. Then she directs her anger into her acting. This time the speech is different, cynical and bitter about men.*

BARRY. 'Sir, you mistake; 'tis not my love I blame,
But my discretion: here the active flame
Should yet a longer time have been concealed;

Too soon, too soon I fear it was revealed.
Our weaker sex glories in surprise,
We boast the sudden conquests of our eyes:
But men esteem a foe that dares contend,
One that with noble courage does defend
A wounded heart; the victories men gain
They prize by their own hazard and their pain.'

Pause.

Well? Was there improvement?

ROCHESTER. Did you think so?

BARRY. I wish to know *your* thoughts.

ROCHESTER. It was better, but now you're too damned angry.

BARRY. Of course I'm fucking angry! You walk into this
theatre in your thirty-shilling boots and tell me how I should
set about my work. I warn you now I have a temper and have
been known to strike out with the first object to hand and if it
be a property blade, well, some have sharper edges than is
needful so have a care.

ROCHESTER. To die on stage at the hands of a lovely woman –

BARRY. I am no such!

ROCHESTER. I think I can make you an actress of truth, not a
creature of artifice. I can do this, but I cannot train you
unless you give a little towards me.

BARRY. It is not in my nature to give. I have my talent and I am
jealous of it, and though I give you credit that you alone in all
the town have seen it, I am not so dazzled by the lord and
master in you that I cannot resent you. Yes, you are right, I am
intent on doing something that no other has yet done and I lost
my purpose yesterday with fear of the Pit, but I will conquer
them and it shall not be said when I have my fame and my two
pound a week – I am worth no less – that Lord Rochester
touched me with the shining wing of his genius and so made
me into a little corner of his greatness, NO, I shall be valued
for me, and for what I knew I could do upon this stage and

how I, Lizzie Barry, took the heat of my own soul and moulded it into a wondrous thing and so triumphed.

ROCHESTER. If I can help you to that triumph, I am not so devoted to the trumpeting of my works that I would wish to take credit –

BARRY. So you say now. But in the alehouse, when the play is done and the talk is of my Cleopatra, will you not slide towards your cronies with an 'I taught her that piece of business' or 'She could not be heard in the gallery till I instructed her in a trick or two.'

ROCHESTER. Madam. I offer my services. If you see no advantage in them, they can as easy be withdrawn.

BARRY. You can buy my slit for a pound a night, sir. I would not mind that, but I think you would not have it so. What I think you want is power over me which I do bridle at, for it is only *I* can make myself into what you say I can be, and if you wish to play a part in this, I would strongly know why.

ROCHESTER. Ask yourself what you want from the theatre.

BARRY. I want the passionate love of my audience. I want, when I make a sweep of my arm, to carry their hearts away, and when I die that they should sigh for never seeing me again – till the next afternoon.

ROCHESTER. There is your answer. I want to be one of that multitude. I wish to be moved. I cannot feel in life, I must have others do it for me here.

BARRY. You are spoken of as a man with a stomach for life.

ROCHESTER. I am the cynic of our golden age. This bounteous dish which our Great Charles and our Great God have – in more or less equal measure – placed before us sets my teeth permanently on edge. Life has no purpose, it is everywhere undone by arbitrariness: I do this, but it matters not a jot if I do the opposite. But in the playhouse, every action good or bad has its consequence; drop a handkerchief and it will return to smother you. Outside the playhouse there are for me no crimes and no consequences.

BARRY. Except in the eyes of God.

ROCHESTER. God is a thing men have made to frighten themselves with. Once frightened, they find meaning, like children playing in the scarecrow's field. Well, I am not to be frightened. I have shied my stones at the scarecrow, it is struck down and I am not.

BARRY. But you are not content.

ROCHESTER. Contentment is the drug of fools. I prefer truth. And the truth is that we are animals scratching and rutting under an empty sky. Here in this theatre we can pretend that our lives have meaning. But the pretence only holds if we are given the truth. That is why I wish to see you shine on this stage, that is why, selfishly, I wish to train you. The theatre is my soothing drug, and my cynic's illness is so far advanced that my physic must be of the highest quality.

BARRY. Well, my lord. Upon those terms, I shall endeavour to do what you want.

ROCHESTER. What I want, is that we meet again tomorrow to consider Ophelia.

BARRY. This is all for a wager, is it not? I am a filly you have put your shirt on.

ROCHESTER. You are a damnably suspicious one.

BARRY. Ophelia then, if you wish. But do not neglect the lesson of Mr Etherege's speech.

ROCHESTER. And what is that?

BARRY. That women should ever treat men with suspicion.

ROCHESTER. I am happy to return and address our work with that instruction written on the inside of my skull.

BARRY. Well then, tomorrow.

ROCHESTER. We'll study the mad scene. I would have you mad. I shall pick up some flowers from the market.

ROCHESTER *goes.* LUSCOMBE *comes on, shouting.*

LUSCOMBE. Bring in the curtain for *Tamburlaine*. Lizzie, you will get off my stage before I strike you.

BARRY. Yes.

BARRY does not move. LUSCOMBE looks at her.

LUSCOMBE. You have not, I hope, made an enemy?

BARRY. I trust I have not made a friend.

The lights fade quickly. ROCHESTER *returns with a bottle.*

ROCHESTER. What was that? I had travelled Europe, fought in a pair of desperate actions at sea, scribbled, gawped, railed and retched at the indistinguishable beauties and horrors of the world in search of some meaningful sensation, and, at last, I had succeeded. To arrive on the scene a Goliath and to quit it reeling, clutching the head, the heart, the cods, unsure where the stone had hit, but sensing in every part its fatal sting. Something in Elizabeth Barry's manner spoke with great certainty of the final four-poster. But there was one place in London which dedicated itself to the cauterising even of such desperate wounds as these and my topboots knew the way of their own volition. They followed the path to Dog and Bitch Yard.

The lights fade around him.

Scene Five – The Imperfect Enjoyment

Dog and Bitch Yard. Very dark. A quality of nightmare.
WHORES *are touting for* CLIENTS.

WHORE 1. Five shillings.

PUNTER. Front or back?

WHORE 2. Front, back –

WHORE 1. Anything you can find in between –

WHORE 2. Long as you got five.

PUNTER. I got four.

WHORE 1. Four you can frig your famble.

WHORE 2. Privy licker!

   ROCHESTER *comes in.*

ROCHESTER. Jane! Jane! Are you there?

MADAM (*off*). Who wants her?

ROCHESTER. You know who I am.

MADAM. Oh, my lord, we are honoured.

WHORE 1. Gent of the Royal Bedchamber!

WHORE 2. Royal Bedpan!

ROCHESTER. Where's Jane?

MADAM (*off*). Becky's free, won't she do?

WHORE 2. I'm free an' all.

ROCHESTER. I want my Jane.

MADAM (*off*). They're never 'my', Johnny. Should know that.

ROCHESTER. While I'm having her she is my Jane. And I never
   think of her any other way. So in my head she is my Jane.

BOUNCER (*off*). Who the fuck is that?

MADAM. Shut your row!

BOUNCER (*off*). If he wants to toss himself off in the passage, let him do it quietly.

ROCHESTER. Who said that? Who's there?

JANE (*off*). Johnny, is that you?

ROCHESTER. Jane.

MADAM. Happy now?

Dimly we see JANE.

JANE. I am glad you're back in London.

ROCHESTER. Missed me?

JANE. I missed the money.

ROCHESTER. Good. Don't like a whore with sentiment. I like a transaction.

JANE. Course you do. He was here earlier.

ROCHESTER. Who?

JANE. The King.

ROCHESTER. Old Rowley? Does he not get enough knobbing off the State without having to pay?

JANE. Everyone likes to pay.

ROCHESTER. It's not his money.

JANE. Don't come over Republican, Johnny. It don't suit a gent with houses in the country.

ROCHESTER. Do you ever do him?

JANE. Sometimes.

ROCHESTER. You go to the Palace?

JANE. There's a back staircase.

ROCHESTER. I'll pay for anything you can get on him.

JANE. What for?

ROCHESTER. He wants me to write a play. I've decided I'm going to do it. But he will be the hero of the piece.

JANE. I'll listen. But only if you let me be in it.

ROCHESTER. You wouldn't want that.

JANE. Wouldn't I?

ROCHESTER. Do me.

JANE. Do you how?

ROCHESTER. Mouth.

JANE. Feeling rough?

ROCHESTER *gives* JANE *money.*

ROCHESTER. Just do it, mouth.

JANE. You only want mouth when there's something wrong.

ROCHESTER. It's a transaction. Give me mouth.

JANE *goes down on him. We can see almost nothing.*

CHARLES. Johnny!

ROCHESTER. Who's there?

CHARLES. 'My sceptre and my prick are of a length.'

ROCHESTER. Your Majesty.

CHARLES. Nice to see your wife in London.

ROCHESTER. I'm just trying to take a nice quiet gobble.

CHARLES. I'm up Big Dolly, do you fancy a swap?

ROCHESTER. Oh God.

CHARLES. John? I'll leave you alone if you want. Glad you're back.

ROCHESTER. Thanks.

CHARLES. Come and have a drink with me at Whitehall tomorrow.

ROCHESTER. I thought it was all serious from now.

CHARLES. No harm in a drink. Bring the boys, I get bored with politics after seven o'clock.

ROCHESTER. I'll bring the boys.

BIG DOLLY. Oh, *vivat rex. Vivat rex carolus.*

CHARLES. Thank you, Dolly! One day I'll make you a duchess.

Pause.

JANE. Gone. Am I still supposed to be doing this?

ROCHESTER. Give it your best, Jane.

She sucks him. Some moments.

'Trembling, confused, despairing, limber, dry,
A wishing, weak unmoving lump I lie.
This dart of love, whose piercing point, oft tried,
With virgin blood ten thousand maids have dyed;
Now languid lies in this unhappy hour,
Shrunk up and sapless, like a withered flower.'

JANE. What you say?

ROCHESTER. Just quoting myself.

JANE. I have the feeling this is going nowhere.

ROCHESTER. I have that feeling too.

JANE. Not like you, John.

ROCHESTER. I met this woman. That new actress. Lizzie Barry.

JANE. Her? She ain't no looker.

ROCHESTER. There is… spirit in her.

JANE. Oh, gawd. John, when you start looking for the spirit and not the eyes or the tits, then a gent is in trouble, believe me.

ROCHESTER. Button me. I am not the man I was wont to be.

JANE. It's nothing. You're still the king of 'em all, just you been drinking tonight.

ROCHESTER. I've been drinking for three years. I blame Thomas Hobbes.

JANE. Innkeeper?

ROCHESTER. Philosopher. Effect's much the same. Would you call me a cynic, Jane?

JANE. I would call you a man who pretends to like life more than he does.

ROCHESTER. Is that a cynic?

JANE. I'm just a moll-sack, I don't do questions.

ROCHESTER. If I am a cynic… how have I fallen in love with a plain woman whom I do not know?

JANE. You saw her on stage. All the colours and the poems they say. Gives 'em a glow. You seen her out of the theatre?

ROCHESTER. No.

JANE. There, that's you then. They say men fall three times. First is calf love.

ROCHESTER. Ah yes –

JANE. Second is the one you marry. Third…

ROCHESTER. Yes?

JANE. Third… is your deathbed bride. Sniff her, sniff your own shroud.

ROCHESTER. How you have cheered me, my dear.

JANE. John. Go home, sleep and forget.

ROCHESTER. Don't want to sleep.

JANE. Go home, lie down and think.

ROCHESTER. Don't want to think. Don't ever want to think again. Here, have some money.

JANE. You give me already.

ROCHESTER. Then I give you again.

ROCHESTER *goes. A dim light comes up on* JANE.

JANE. I hate it when they try to make you care for them. Like they have more to fret over than you do, some hoping. I rather he had come his fetch all over my face than he had left me with this lump of caring for him. A little buzz in the brain saying 'Johnny ain't himself.' Oh, I can use him, a girl can raise herself on the hook she stakes in an earl. But I will not be burdened with his buzz.

Lights fade quickly to blackout.

Scene Six – Portrait

ROCHESTER's *London lodgings.* JACOB HUYSMANS *is making sketches for a portrait of* ROCHESTER *and* MALET.

MALET. I remembered in the night why I do not care for London. I go to bed alone at half past nine and am woken a little after one o'clock by a frenzied kicking and pushing and snatching of covers. He smells of his drink and his harlot and then he badgers me with his love. It is such a sorrowful love it makes the heart of me weep. He is so sorry that he has inflicted his drink and harlot on me. I do not care. I would not care if he brought drink, harlot and laddish companions into the bed so long as he was not sorry. If he could have the pleasure he had paid for and come to me, not contrite but satiated, all would be bearable. But he has paid out money and his own lifeblood and has not had pleasure of his pleasure. And he must needs wake me and tell me how miserable a thing was his debauche and how much he would have preferred to spend the evening in my arms. But the next day all is forgotten. Off he forages again and the one o'clock performance is repeated until I can bear it no longer and return to Adderbury where the quiet of growing trees and the running of a large house and estate and the children compensate loneliness. In the country it is different. We go to bed together and he smells of dogs and horses. And there is no sorrow in his love.

General lighting comes up.

ROCHESTER. I do so hate London. I wish we were back in the country.

MALET. You must not speak, my dear, you render Mr Huysman's task so difficult.

ROCHESTER. Only if, at the moment I spoke, he happened to be drawing my mouth.

MALET. It is not just your mouth, John. You become animated on the topic of your choice and are then perpetually at fidget.

ROCHESTER. Except that I was speaking of the country, a subject on which it is very hard to be animated.

MALET. You said that you loved it.

ROCHESTER. There are many forms of love. Love of the country is passive, eh, Mr Huysmans? You lie back and it does things to you.

MALET. Do not distract, my dear.

ROCHESTER. Looking out of that window, when occasion permits me to do, I cannot but note that organ-grinder and his monkey and the pair they make together.

MALET. Animation again, John, hush yourself.

Pause.

ROCHESTER. Could you not say something, Mr Huysmans? By way of breaking the silence.

HUYSMANS. I am working on your eyes. This is an operation as delicate as surgery on the retina. Particularly since your right eye is the eye of an innocent schoolboy while your left is the eye of a man who has recently awoken in a sewer.

ROCHESTER. Shall I run him through with my sword, Elizabeth?

MALET. Stay still, my love.

ALCOCK *enters with wine*. ROCHESTER *has his back to*
ALCOCK *but immediately becomes aware of the presence*
of drink.

ROCHESTER. Ah. Is that the good Alcock?

ALCOCK. It is, my lord.

ROCHESTER. Bearing strong drink.

ALCOCK. Indeed, my lord.

ROCHESTER *sniffs.*

ROCHESTER. Claret. Mr Huysmans, would you permit a short
interlude?

HUYSMANS. In five minutes' time.

ROCHESTER (*anxious*). In five minutes. (*Pause.*) Here's
another thought, Mr Huysmans. Perhaps a bottle and glass
would be a handsome adornment to your composition.

HUYSMANS. They are not appropriate objects in a family
portrait, my lord.

ROCHESTER. Could they not become so? This is the age of
experiment after all.

MALET. No.

ROCHESTER. Here's another thought, Huysmans, I have an
excellent composition in mind, better than this one. I very
much wish you to paint it for me sometime. You see that
monkey yonder, dancing with the organ-grinder. If you have
observed these creatures, you cannot fail to notice how
human they are. My conceit is this: to sit the monkey upon a
pile of solemn volumes and for him to hold in his hand a
scrap of paper, as if it were a poem he has just written, d'you
see? And while he is offering me the poem, I am crowning
him with the bays: is that not a most excellent fancy?

HUYSMANS. I find Lady Rochester a more elegant and
interesting subject.

ROCHESTER. You are wide of the point, sir. Elegance, interest, all very well in their way, but what do they illuminate? We can all hide underneath periwigs and extravagant dresses and discourse of the Italian gardening tradition, but what *are* we?

MALET. Am I not, then, an apt partner for you to sit with?

ROCHESTER. You have missed the thrust of my remark. It is no matter.

MALET. Am I not apt?

ROCHESTER. You are apt, Elizabeth, you are very apt.

MALET. But you would prefer a monkey?

> ROCHESTER *stands suddenly and snatches a glass of claret from the tray. He drinks it in one gulp and, when* ALCOCK *refills it, snatches the glass and carries on drinking.*

You would rather be painted with a monkey?

ROCHESTER. Really, Elizabeth, it is of a muchness. You are both very apt in your different ways.

MALET. And wherein does my aptness lie?

ROCHESTER. It was a flippant observation –

MALET. In flippant observation we may find much truth –

ROCHESTER. We laugh at the monkey because its tricks are so close to ours. Human affairs are carried on at such a nonsensical rate that I think it a fault to laugh at the monkey when I compare his condition with mankind. We sit here in our finery so that our grandchildren can point us out to strangers, but it does not tell the truth. In this portrait I am no better than a monkey who knows the name of his ancestors.

MALET. And I?

ROCHESTER. A gaudy female monkey, gloating over the opulence of your cage.

> MALET *goes abruptly.* HUYSMANS *follows.*

I love London. Everyone catches its generous spirit so quickly. I do not mean to upset people, Alcock, it is not a plan I carry around with me, but I have to speak my mind, because what is in my mind is *always* more interesting than what is happening in the world outside my mind, and if I cannot connect the two, I will become mad, d'you see?

ALCOCK. It makes you impossible to live with, though, d'you see?

ROCHESTER. Alcock, did I praise you for your blunt manner?

ALCOCK. I think it was your reason for employing me, sir.

ROCHESTER. Good, don't forget that. I shall endeavour to retrace the footsteps of the conversation with my wife.

He is about to go, then turns back to ALCOCK.

But do you not remember the way Mrs Barry looked on stage?

'Your kindness gave my yeelding spirits rest,
And rais'd me to a dwelling in your brest.'

ALCOCK. You should not think playhouse thoughts, my lord.

ROCHESTER. These last two days, playhouse thoughts are all the thoughts I have had.

ALCOCK. Go to your wife, my lord.

ROCHESTER. I'll be obliged for the rest of that claret before I obey your orders.

ALCOCK *gives* ROCHESTER *the rest of the bottle.*

D'you know, a dog bit me on the leg in Covent Garden while I was reeling in this morning. I felt such ill will to the creature that I wished it married and living in the country. Alcock?

ALCOCK. My lord.

ROCHESTER. Do it.

MALET *comes in.* ALCOCK *goes.*

MALET. If I had mighty hopes of our marriage, it was because you were so impassioned that you abducted me and went to the Tower for it. I had never expected so much of a man. I was not to know that this would be the best gesture of your love.

ROCHESTER. It was the most hot-headed.

MALET. It was the best. It made me believe it was me you wanted and not my estate.

ROCHESTER. I carved your name on the wall of my cell. Though had you been a pauper, my love would have been more severely tested.

MALET. I could bear more easily the marriages of other wealthy ladies I have witnessed. For there to be no pretence of passion or affection, to be merely a housekeeper and a conduit for the noble line. But when you are away from me you write so beguilingly of how you miss me. And so my feelings are kept in play only to be shunned and spurned on our reunion. I do not think you mean to torture me, but it is a torture to be informed of passion at a distance and then in the flesh to be so reviled.

ROCHESTER. You know I always mean it to be well when we are together. But after a few weeks I find I have no gift for it. In my mind I am somewhere else.

MALET. Then cut me out of your heart completely and have done. I think you only hold on to me to remind yourself that you once did have such a thing as a heart. You despise the King and his politics, you hurl your lampoons at the Court and your companions and you turn your back on God. Do not except me from your contempt any longer, treat me the way you treat the rest of the world.

He holds her.

ROCHESTER. Do not command me to do something beyond my power.

MALET. Sometimes I fall to thinking. Is the fault to be laid at my door? Were I a better wife, you would have a better character. You would not need the whorehouse and the inn –

ROCHESTER. There is no man born has no need of the whorehouse and the inn –

MALET. It is sin, John. I know you despise me when I speak in this way, but you are daily worn away by sin and ungodliness. You turned your back on God for the same reason you turn your back on the King. Because you cannot allow of a power which is stronger than yourself. When one day you discover your own weakness, you will change your mind and perhaps become a more supportable companion.

Suddenly BARRY *bursts in. She is dressed as a ragged Ophelia and carries some mangy flowers.*

BARRY. There's rosemary, that's for rememberance; pray you, love, remember: and there's pansies that's for thoughts. (*To* MALET.) There's fennel for you, and columbines; (*To* ROCHESTER.) There's rue for you and here's some for me: we may call it herb of grace o' Sundays: O you must wear your rue with a difference. There's a daisy: I would give you some violets but they had none down the market and in any case you are not faithful, so it would not be fitting. For if you may walk into my world, I may surely walk into yours and be as great a nuisance to you as you have been to me.

BARRY *goes.*

MALET. How refreshing is the company in this town. She is a playhouse creature, is she not?

ROCHESTER. Actress.

MALET. And when your eyes shone the other day, they were shining for her.

ROCHESTER. They were.

MALET. I see that I am even more of an obstacle to your life in London than I had supposed. I shall go upstairs and set Jenny to packing right away. I will be gone by the morning.

MALET *goes.* HUYSMANS *returns.*

HUYSMANS. Your man asked that I return to draw you alone.

ROCHESTER. Craving your indulgence, yes. If you are working upon my eyes, why then, my wife may take her rest.

HUYSMAN. If that is your wish, then that is how I shall work.

Some moments, then ALCOCK *comes on. He carries a monkey and places it next to* ROCHESTER.

Excellent fellow, Alcock. How much did the organ-grinder require?

ALCOCK. I gave him ten pound.

ROCHESTER. Ten pound. The fellow has parted with his lifelong companion for the price of a periwig. Is there not a lesson there, gentlemen? Please, Mr Huysmans. Immortalise us.

HUYSMANS *draws. The lights fade around him.*

HUYSMANS. The monkey would not sit still. It soiled beyond repair four handsome volumes of Pliny the Elder and shredded much of Sir Philip Sidney. It was a mean and loathsome afternoon's work. And yet, that winter when I finally finished the portrait in my studio, I was struck by its truth. Of all those bewigged men I painted, bothering posterity with their long faces, he is the only one aware of his own absurdity.

Blackout.

Scene Seven – Sundial

Midnight. Whitehall Gardens. To one side of the stage is CHARLES'*s favourite sundial, an expensive, phallic object. Some drunken cavorting off, then* CHARLES, ROCHESTER, SACKVILLE *and* DOWNS *come on.*

CHARLES. So I said to her, 'I don't care which duchess you are, you're not bringing my horse into your bedchamber.'

They all laugh.

Thus far will I go with you, gentlemen, and no further.

ROCHESTER. The fresh air begins to dander up his cods.

CHARLES. My wits, my sparks, we have caroused, have we not!

DOWNS. We have.

ROCHESTER. Poor Nelly, just drifting off and the great royal nudger shoves you from the arms of Morphius.

CHARLES. But you know the difference between us. At seven I'll be on the tennis court and by eight I'll be running the country again. (*To* ROCHESTER.) Where will you be, John?

ETHEREGE *comes on.*

ROCHESTER. I shall be in my married bed, striving to become your conscious subject.

CHARLES. I wish you well of it. Goodnight, gentlemen.

CHARLES *goes.*

ETHEREGE. Goodnight, Your Majesty.

ROCHESTER. Give Nelly one from all of us.

DOWNS. The King! I took wine with the King!

SACKVILLE. You talk of Nelly, but you don't know. I had her. And before he did.

ROCHESTER. Anon it starts.

DOWNS. He called me Billy and talked to me on the subject of fob watches.

SACKVILLE. Seventeen years old!

DOWNS. And he listened to what I said. How I always wind mine up using the thumb and third finger. Nodded as if I had spluttered something sage.

SACKVILLE. Such hair!

ROCHESTER. The skin, lactescent in all probability.

SACKVILLE. Her skin... how was it... skin... lactescent!!

ROCHESTER. Someone do something with him. George.

SACKVILLE. I suckled there, like a hog at a trough!

ROCHESTER. He's turning my stomach.

ETHEREGE. Come on, Charlie, let's go to Dog and Bitch Yard. That nice Dolly Mossop'll snatch frig you, you'll just about manage that.

SACKVILLE. I don't want Dolly Mossop, I want my Nell.

DOWNS. I'll have Dolly Mossop. Has anyone got any money?

ROCHESTER. George'll pay, George makes money out of writing. Not exactly something a real gentleman should do, of course, make money out of writing, like sending your wife out to sell oranges –

SACKVILLE. It's too late to go and fuck Dolly Mossop.

DOWNS. How can it be too late?

SACKVILLE. By now she'll be into double figures. I hate it when they smell more of man than they do of woman.

DOWNS. Late? It's not late.

SACKVILLE. It is late.

ETHEREGE. John! Johnny!! What time is it?

SACKVILLE. What time is it? You're standing next to the most sophisticated timepiece in Europe, you tell me.

ROCHESTER. It's a *sundial*, shufflehead, we're in the dark.

ETHEREGE. M'Lord Buckhurst does a good impression of the sun, don't you, Chas?

DOWNS. He does what?

ETHEREGE. Go on, Chas, spread your little beams.

   SACKVILLE *imitates the sun. He improvises verse.*

SACKVILLE. 'Behold I am Phoebus, light's speedy chariot:
Harbinger of day, I put dark night to rout:
My silver beams that speed through night's thick cloak
Do something something in that realm of smoke.'

ROCHESTER. And he thinks Dryden's bad.

SACKVILLE. 'Creatures of earth, I bring thee heat and light
I make the milkmaid and the king alike seem bright – '

DOWNS. Brighter, brighter.

ETHEREGE. Still can't tell the time.

SACKVILLE. 'Great though thou art, pale moon – '

ROCHESTER. Chas!

ETHEREGE. It's not working, Chas. You did well, but –

ROCHESTER (*approaching the sundial*). Let me peruse this device, I am not so much in addled alley as the rest of you... quarter past, five and twenty... I can't read it...

ETHEREGE. Johnny –

ROCHESTER. What the *fuck* is wrong with this sundial?

ETHEREGE. Steady, Johnny.

ROCHESTER. He calls himself King!! The greatest patron of the arts and sciences in Europe. The nimble mind, bounding with ease from subject to subject. Cunt spends sixty thousand pounds on a clock and it doesn't work in the dark.

ETHEREGE. Come on, Johnny.

   ROCHESTER *snaps a bit of the sundial off. There is an awful, sobering silence.*

   Look, we'll slip away, it's just a bit of metal, could have been anyone –

SACKVILLE. Could have been a gust –

ETHEREGE. Johnny –

ROCHESTER. I hate this thing. I hate the way it stands here fucking the sky, fucking time. So you've got a big dick, Charlie, why ram it down our throats all the time? Isn't it enough that you're the King? Must there be nothing left for anyone else?

DOWNS. He wants the lot.

ETHEREGE. Look, I'm off home, got this committee tomorrow morning –

ROCHESTER. ARE WE GENTLEMEN OR ARE WE NOT? Are we prepared to see our monarch ravishing the rosy maiden time with his big glass whatsit?

DOWNS. I'm with you.

ROCHESTER. Tumble it down!

ETHEREGE. No.

ROCHESTER. TUMBLE IT DOWN!!

ROCHESTER draws his sword and launches it at the sundial. DOWNS joins in.

DOWNS. Tumble the King down!

ROCHESTER. Down with Time and Kings!

SACKVILLE picks up the mood and slashes at the sundial.

SACKVILLE. King Time, down!!!

ROCHESTER. Kings and kingdoms tumble down and so shall thou!

ETHEREGE joins in. They all start jumping up and down on the smashed bits.

ALL. Kings and kingdoms tumble down, tumble down, tumble down,
Kings and kingdoms tumble down,
AND SO SHALL THOU!!!

The alarm is raised off. A GUARD shouts.

ETHEREGE. Someone's seen us.

SACKVILLE. Johnny? Come on, Johnny.

SACKVILLE runs off. DOWNS follows. ROCHESTER seems oblivious. ETHEREGE tries to drag him off.

ETHEREGE. Come on, Johnny, end of caper.

ROCHESTER. I haven't finished!

ETHEREGE. The guard's spotted us.

ROCHESTER. I wish to trample his dick to dust, George, don't interrupt me!

ETHEREGE *does his best to manhandle* ROCHESTER *off, but* ROCHESTER *shoves him away.* ETHEREGE *escapes.*

Kings and kingdoms tumble down and so shall thou!

The sundial is dust.

And so shall thou. And so shall thou.

A GUARD *comes on with sword drawn.*

No use waving your porker now, fellow, you've missed them! That way, that way.

The GUARD *looks bemused for a second, then rushes off in pursuit of the* WITS.

Time is but dust, and kings, and me also, the body maggoting so soon, so soon after I was godlike and sturdy. My legs ache in the morning and my brain is the dinner of a slow ruminating beast.

A noise off. ROCHESTER *hears but doesn't look.*

All right. Take me away in chains. I admit. I did it. Whatever is the King's pleasure shall be mine. I must always go too far, you see, it is my genius to go too far.

A cloaked figure comes on. It's BARRY.

BARRY. My lord. (*Pause.*) What passed between us this afternoon when I came as Ophelia. If I surprised you and made as if to push you away, it was only a try at coming towards you.

She wraps her cloak and herself around him.

You have been all this time with the King and I have been waiting.

ROCHESTER. Lizzie!

BARRY. Cold. Are you not cold?

ROCHESTER. No longer.

BARRY. Was there not something here at one time? Some monument?

ROCHESTER. No, not here. There was nothing here till now.

They embrace voluptuously.

Blackout.

Interval.

Scene Eight – Sodom

Lights up on a CHORUS OF WOMEN*: all hold enormous dildoes. They sing and dance the following:*

WOMEN. You ladies all of merry England
    Who have been to kiss the Duchess's hand,
    Pray, did you lately observe in the show
    A noble Italian called Signior Dildo?

    This signior was one of Her Highness's train,
    And help'd to conduct her over the main;
    But now she cries out, 'To the Duke I will go!
    I have no more need of Signior Dildo.'

    At the sign of the cross in St James's Street,
    When next you go thither to make yourself sweet
    By buying of powder, gloves, essence, or so,
    You may chance t'get a sight of Signior Dildo.

    My Lady Southesk, heavens prosper her for't!
    First clothed him in satin, then brought him to Court
    But his head in the circle he scarcely durst show,
    So modest a youth was Signior Dildo.

    Our dainty fine duchesses have got a trick
    To dote on a fool for the sake of his prick:
    The fops were undone, did their Graces but know
    The discretion and vigor of Signior Dildo.

This Signior is sound, safe ready and dumb
As ever was candle, carrot, or thumb;
Then away with these nasty devices and show
How you rate the just merits of Signior Dildo.

Lights up on Windsor Great Park. ROCHESTER is
rehearsing his play Sodom. BARRY, JANE *and* HARRIS
stand by. ALCOCK *looks on.* LUSCOMBE *makes notes.*

ROCHESTER. Now. We have a bare four hours before we
present my Major Work of Literature to the King, so let us
not sloven. Act Two, Scene Three: 'The scene changes and
discovers the Queen in a chair of state.'

LUSCOMBE. What kind of chair was that you were wanting?

ROCHESTER. Molly, I am trying to rehearse the actresses.

LUSCOMBE. And I am making sure that you have what you
want, because if you don't, then I know there will be roaring,
swearing and breaking of furniture and heads which I would
not like to be mine.

ROCHESTER. Four legs, a seat, a back. Now, Lizzie, you will
please continue in the part of the Queen.

BARRY. I shall make myself comfortable here.

BARRY *settles on a bench.*

ROCHESTER. Thank you, Lizzie... 'and is frigg'd by the lady
Officina' – that's you, Jane.

JANE *takes up a position close to* BARRY.

' – all the rest pulling out their dildoes and frig in point of
honour.'

LUSCOMBE. Who is to be all the rest?

ROCHESTER. Mr Downs and Mr Etherege are even now
recruiting some young women of Windsor to fill these trifling
parts. For the moment, Molly, you will play Fuckadilla –

LUSCOMBE. I am not a visible person, my lord. I am a behind-
the-scenes, invisible kind of person.

ROCHESTER. It's only for this rehearsal, my dear Moll.
Heaven cannot have provided two more assiduous procurers
than Mr Etherege and Mr Downs and they will shortly arrive
laden with Berkshire beauties.

JANE. But who is to be little Clytoris?

ROCHESTER. Clytoris is silent in this scene. Perhaps, Alcock,
you could stand in her place to remind us she is there.

ALCOCK. No, my lord.

ROCHESTER. I beg your pardon.

ALCOCK. My lord, I am Alcock. Little Clytoris is beyond
my range.

ROCHESTER. Alcock! If I command you to impersonate
temporarily the seat of pleasure for the whole of womankind
I do not expect you to demur.

ALCOCK. Very well, my lord. But it must be understood that I
play Clytoris under sufferance.

ALCOCK *drags himself onstage*.

LUSCOMBE. May I formulate a small question at this juncture?

ROCHESTER. Yes, Molly.

LUSCOMBE. Are these the dildoes we will be using for the
performance?

ROCHESTER. They are inadequate. I will provide more
suitable items from my personal collection.

JANE. It is a very fine collection.

LUSCOMBE. I am relieved to hear those words.

HARRIS. I am not in this scene?

ROCHESTER. You are not, Mr Harris, but if you can watch and
learn, I shall be indebted. Shall we make a start?

ETHEREGE *and* DOWNS *come on*.

DOWNS. We're most damnably, miserably sorry, Johnny.

ETHEREGE. Couldn't do it. Simply couldn't find one Windsor
wanton, never mind two who might fit the bill.

ROCHESTER *is very angry.*

ROCHESTER. I NEED TWO MORE WOMEN.

ETHEREGE. Bawds are as much out of fashion as gentleman
ushers.

ROCHESTER. WHAT ARE YOU FOR? Drinking, cursing,
smoking, quarrelling and, *supra omnia*, wenching are the
attributes of your kind of gentleman –

DOWNS. Windsor is a *quiet* town, my lord –

ROCHESTER. Alcock, you're on. And you, Molly. For a brief
hour, you will loom into the range of human sight. Do not
cross me further, anyone. The scene! 'The Queen is frigged
by Lady Officina, all the rest pulling out their dildoes and
frig in point of honour.'

The WOMEN *prepare themselves.*

BARRY. 'So no more yet. You do not make it spirt –
You frig, as if you were afraid to hurt.'

JANE. 'Madam, the fault in Virtuoso lies.' Who is Virtuoso?

LUSCOMBE. Just say the lines.

ROCHESTER. Virtuoso is the merkin and dildo-maker to the
Royal Family, a secure position of employment, I believe.

JANE. 'Madam, the fault in Virtuoso lies
He should have made it of a longer size.
This dildo by a hand full is too short.'

ETHEREGE. And she should know.

BARRY. 'Let him with speed to send for to the Court.'

LUSCOMBE. 'Madam, your dildoes are not to compare
With what I've seen – '

JANE. 'Indeed they're paltry ware.'

LUSCOMBE. 'Short dildoes leave the pleasure half undone.'

JANE. Um, my lord, sorry for stopping, but I'm a bit confused –

ROCHESTER. Yes, Jane –

JANE. I don't understand how we frig 'in point of honour'.

ETHEREGE. Just frig yourself, dear.

JANE. But if we are to frig ourselves in point of honour, is that not a different mode of frigging?

ETHEREGE. Frigging is frigging.

ROCHESTER. The stage direction is a kind of literary joke, to amuse the reader.

HARRIS. It's a play.

JANE. Yes, the audience won't get it, will they?

ROCHESTER. Sometimes an author will indulge himself with his stage directions, writing something which he knows cannot be literally achieved on the stage but with the hope of suggesting a subtle nuance for the solitary reader in the study.

HARRIS. Ah, Lord Rochester, I am glad you said that, because I wished to pose such a question about the final stage direction in this very scene.

ROCHESTER. Yes?

HARRIS. Well, presumably, this direction is similar to the one to which Jane just referred. I mean where it is not possible in performance.

ROCHESTER. It seems straightforward enough.

HARRIS (*reading script*). 'Then dance six naked men and women, the men doing obedience to the women's cunts, kissing and touching them often, the women in like manner to the men's pricks, kissing and dandling their codds, and then fall to fucking, after which the women sigh and the men look simple and so sneak off. The End of the Second Act.'

ETHEREGE *applauds*.

ROCHESTER. A strong scene, an eminently playable scene and though I say it myself, a climactic one.

ETHEREGE. Ha!

HARRIS. In my mind it raises a question.

ROCHESTER. Yes, Mr Harris?

HARRIS. My question is in two parts, the necessity of posing the second being dependent on your answer to the first –

ROCHESTER. Please continue, Mr Harris –

HARRIS. Will the equipment from your private collection of which you spoke be available to the gentlemen for strapping around the middle in the execution of this scene?

ROCHESTER. No, no. I had not envisaged you to be so encumbered, Mr Harris. I feel the scene should be given, so to speak, in the flesh.

HARRIS. Well, it would seem my second question is necessary after all: is it envisaged that we will give two performances of the entertainment on the King's birthday?

ROCHESTER. No, Mr Harris.

HARRIS. I am glad to hear that from the author.

ROCHESTER. With the dress rehearsal, the Court performance and the public showing, I envisage three.

HARRIS *weighs this.*

HARRIS. I don't know if you have met my regular understudy, Mr Lightman, but he is a most dependable fellow –

ROCHESTER. I am delighted to hear it –

HARRIS. And I feel it may be as well –

ROCHESTER. We are being a little forward here. At the moment we are simply preparing a reading of the play for the King's approval. Once we have earned this regal approbation, then we are in a position to discuss furniture, dildoes and understudies for actors who feel the demands of the scene may be beyond them.

Suddenly CHARLES *appears.*

CHARLES. You're here. Don't stop on my account. I do so love the theatre and it is next to impossible to find any in Windsor.

ROCHESTER. Your Majesty, you are a little early, we intend to present the reading to the Court at four o'clock, it is now something short of noon –

CHARLES. Is that so? You know I do have the most *extraordinary* difficulty telling the time these days, can't think why, seem to remember spending *a colossal pile of money* on timepieces a few years ago –

ROCHESTER. Your Majesty, we will be most delighted to perform for you after dinner –

CHARLES. No, no, I am here now. 'Down with Time' say I for one, and I fancy I am not alone in these sentiments.

ROCHESTER. Your Majesty will appreciate our efforts more if –

CHARLES. Fall to. Rehearse. I understand there is to be a representation of a Royal Court. I will be able to assist if there are any blemishes in verisimilitude, wouldn't want that, would we?

ROCHESTER. Your Majesty will be at liberty to make any amendments to the play after the private performance –

CHARLES. Rehearse, I say. I commissioned this play. What's the good of being a patron of the arts if you can't get some when you fancy it, eh?

ROCHESTER. Let us return to the beginning of the dildo scene.

The WOMEN *cluster together.* HARRIS, *off the hook, slopes into a corner.*

CHARLES. Where's this fellow going?

HARRIS. Your Majesty, I am not required in this scene.

CHARLES. But you are to play the King, no?

HARRIS. I am, Your Majesty –

CHARLES. And what is the name of the King?

HARRIS. He is called… Bolloxinion, My Lord. King… of the imaginary Kingdom of Sodom.

CHARLES. Laddy, it may be imaginary to you –

ROCHESTER. There are no scenes, Your Majesty, which Mr Harris can essay without his fellow actors who have been unavoidably detained and will not –

CHARLES. Does this King not have a monologue, a soliloquoy, a prologue or so?

ROCHESTER. He does, Your Majesty.

CHARLES. Well, I would fain hear it. Then I will retire. And let you have more TIME. One speech, Johnny, just to whet the imagination.

Pause.

ROCHESTER. Mr Harris. If you would be so good, let us hear the speech that begins 'Since I have buggered human arse – '

CHARLES. No, no, no. You know the one I want to hear. The one he does at the start of the play, the opening to your Actus Primus, let us hear that.

ROCHESTER. Your Majesty, I do not understand how your familiarity with the work is so great.

CHARLES. Let us hear the speech. And let it be… kingly.

ROCHESTER *nods to* HARRIS. HARRIS, *in agonies, prepares.*

HARRIS. 'Thus in the Zenith of my Lust I reign:
I eat to swive, and swive to eat again;
Let other Monarchs, who their sceptres bear
To keep their subjects less in love than fear,
Be slaves to crowns, my Nation shall be free –
My Pintle only shall my sceptre be;
My laws shall act more pleasure than command
And with my Prick, I'll govern all the land.'

Pause.

CHARLES. It's very good, you know, Johnny, only this fellow ain't kingly enough. You know I have been a King a decent while, a while longer than some people might allow –

He looks around, sniffing Republicans.

– and, what is more, I have knocked around among the kingly sort, and there is a thing you find with your kingly fucker... and that is that your kingly fucker expects to be obeyed, understand, Mr Harris?

HARRIS. Yes, Your Majesty.

CHARLES. But the fellow you showed me there, verged on the NERVY side of kingship, a thing I have observed but little in the regal type, d'y'see?

HARRIS. I do see, Your Majesty –

CHARLES. So let's have it again: 'My laws shall act' and so on.

HARRIS. 'My laws shall act more pleasure than command
And with my prick, I'll govern all the land.'

CHARLES. This portrayal, Mr Harris, would it be based on any particular monarch?

HARRIS *swallows air.*

Or is it more your general notion of majesty you are seeking to pillory?

ROCHESTER. Thank you, ladies, thank you, Mr Harris, the rehearsal is at an end.

No one moves.

CHARLES. Well, you heard the orders of your author. If an author can't get what he wants in his own theatre, it's a damn poor lookout, ain't it?

HARRIS *takes this as a dismissal, bows and exits.* ALL *but* ROCHESTER *follow him.*

ROCHESTER. You commission me to write for you and yet I find I am not trusted.

CHARLES. And I was right. I present you with an opportunity. I command you to seize this chance to fulfil your shining promise. And what do you give me?

CHARLES *takes a copy of the play out of his coat and throws it on the floor.*

A pornographic representation of a Royal Court where the men deal only in buggery and the women's sole object of interest is the dildo.

ROCHESTER. A monument to your reign.

Pause.

CHARLES. You will leave Windsor now. You are prohibited from the precincts of the Court in London. If you show your face, it will be the Tower.

CHARLES *goes.* ROCHESTER *shouts after him.*

ROCHESTER. You are so *limited.* Can you not think of anything else to do to me?

BARRY *comes back on.*

BARRY. He will relent.

ROCHESTER. I don't want him to relent. I want him hurt.

BARRY. Do you care for me at all?

ROCHESTER. I have loved you from the beginning.

BARRY. But thus love does not alter or inspire you.

ROCHESTER. That's not the truth –

BARRY. Then why does it not free you from your past? You mock and batter the King as if he were a father you were doomed forever to enrage. You are diminished by this battle. It holds you back from the sublime. I can pacify the wounded animal in you but you must let me near it. If you loved me you would engage with me.

ROCHESTER. I can now engage with nothing. I am banished and must return to my wife in the country –

BARRY. No, you must not! You will not take the King's
   displeasure as a sign to run from me. Stay close to London
   where I may lay easy hands on you. And I will sue for you to
   the King so he may quickly change his mind.

ROCHESTER. Lizzie? I would be pacified.

She holds out a hand to him. They exit together.

Scene Nine – Epsom

DOWNS. To become a wit, a blade, a spark. The very word,
   spark, a hot splinter of fashion to scorch the town and burn it
   to the ground. There was never another way for me. I live for
   the cocky swagger: toss the head, grind the loins and gob the
   pavings. What though they had kept me two years at my
   Cambridge Latin, learning to parse and wrangle, I came to
   London bent on cutting a figure with the hot boys. A
   lecherous leer to the traffic and a stamp of the boot on the
   alehouse floor: I lived for these Friday-night gestures and
   thought they would satisfy till I was twenty-five and in my
   grave. But to be a part of the merry gang, for Billy Downs to
   hang on the coat-tails of my Lord Rochester and the Earl of
   Dorset, such a thing stood several leagues beyond my
   dreams and I cling to their companionship like an old toper
   to his pottle. My mother writes to me, asks what I am doing
   in this dreadful town. I cannot reply, for there is no setting
   down with ink and paper that I drink till I am sick, mump
   and quarrel till I duel and wench till I am slapped or
   satisfied. I am the youngest of three brothers. The eldest has
   the estate and the second is a canting priest. Between them
   they have done me out of wealth and piety. There is nothing
   left to me but spark, so spark I shall. Today we jolly forth to
   the Epsom Races, and though my jerkin has not the force of
   my companions' topcoats, yet I keep my end up with a clutch
   of lively sallies and modern curses that fan the fading embers
   of their youth.

General lighting comes up. DOWNS *and* ETHEREGE *in a huddle at the racetrack.* SACKVILLE *approaches, breathless.*

ETHEREGE. You lose, lose, lose all afternoon but you must never give up hope.

SACKVILLE. I have the word from the paddock. Danny's on the big grey and he's frisky round the chops.

ETHEREGE. The word from the paddock!

DOWNS. Buggers stable boys for sixpence and they tip him donkeys for vengeance.

SACKVILLE. Ten pounds says the grey's the briskest.

ETHEREGE. Middlesex, fuck you.

DOWNS (*looking off*). Seven to four the grey, fives Vanishing Spark, a hundred to eight the field.

ETHEREGE. I at least have bet like a man, my last thirty pound on the Duke of Newcastle's nag.

ROCHESTER *and* BARRY *come on, arm in arm, utterly involved in each other.*

DOWNS. You're a regular Knight of the Elbow, George. Who's carrying your money, Johnny?

No reaction from ROCHESTER.

SACKVILLE. It queases my guts to see a gent so deep in a baggage.

ETHEREGE. Johnny!

Still nothing from ROCHESTER.

I hate watching love. If I were King I would publish an Act of Parliament limiting the disease to private, windowless rooms.

DOWNS. They're up to the line, they're under orders, and… they're off!!

In the following, SACKVILLE, ETHEREGE, BARRY *and* DOWNS *speak at once,* ROCHESTER *separately.*

ETHEREGE. Not there, not there, no point in being there, get ROUND the grey you can't get THROUGH him –

SACKVILLE. Go, you beauty, don't do too much too soon, hold him back, hold him back, save something for the last furlong, the damned hothead –

BARRY. Oh you are a fine, handsome animal, give me a run for the little coin I have thrown on you, give me a run, you sweetheart fucker –

DOWNS. Go on, Vanishing Spark, go my Spark, go you Sparky Spark, go, go, go, give him the whip, don't just show it to him, make him run for *me* –

ROCHESTER. Why weighs my money on a horse's back so hard?
Thus grac'd, the thoroughbred turns meat for knacker's yard.

ETHEREGE. You are trying to *win*, that is the point, do you not comprehend, simple fact, arrive at winning post ahead of all other animals, you will not do that if you get stuck behind –

SACKVILLE. Oh smooth as silk, as satin, oh yes, Danny, nice move, no, no, no, no, yes, yes, oh you are a whoreson cunning, but watch, watch on the rails, do you not see, ON THE RAILS, are you blind –

BARRY. Why do they match my fine horse with such a tawdry jockey? He is like a monkey on its back. If I were to act as he rides I would be in the street soon enough –

DOWNS. Spark, Spark, Spark, Spark, go, go, no, go, go, where is the run? Where has the run in him gone? Get him go, get him go, Spark, Spark –

ROCHESTER. Doomed with my gold, the jockey, cunning racer Becomes at once a green apprentice chaser.

ETHEREGE. YOU CUNT!! You are doing this deliberately, who has bribed you, you unspeakable, useless shit, you should have dying vermin draped hourly around your genitalia in perpetuity!!

SACKVILLE. OH YOU BEAUTY!! You knew all the time, let him run, let him run, smooth as velvet, smooth as Nelly's cunt, oh you have him, Danny, I could roger you up the bum, you beauty, you beauty, YOU BEAUTY!!

BARRY. Fourth! Can you do no better than that. I do not like to associate myself with something that is fourth. I am aspiring to greatness. Fourth!

DOWNS. Vanishing Spark, go on, Vanishing Spark, go on, go *on*, where, where, where, WHERE IS IT, where is the run, where is the spark, where is the spark gone in you, YOU DISEASE!!

ROCHESTER. Once more the death knell of my hopes is struck and rings
I should expect no better from the sport of kings.

A tableau of victory and defeat, then a change. The last race is over. They are kicking their way back through the day's rubbish.

ETHEREGE. I hate racing, Sport of Kings, sport of peasants –

SACKVILLE. Come on, Georgie, you like it when you win –

ETHEREGE. Must have seen the backside off sixty pound today, could have BOUGHT a horse –

DOWNS. You're ruled by the heart, George, damn bad thing in a sportsman, you *fall* for horses, should be suspicious of them –

SACKVILLE. I'll stand you a fat dinner at the inn if you just stop your whining –

ROCHESTER (*suddenly stops still*). It must have been one of you. Yesterday, with the King. I've just seen it. One of you betrayed me. Yes?

DOWNS. Johnny?

ROCHESTER. Showed a copy to the King. George. It was you, wasn't it?

ETHEREGE. What?

ROCHESTER. Of course. I dispatch you and Billy to search for women but you don't go, instead you take the play to His glorious Majesty –

ETHEREGE. Johnny, much as I like you, I do try not to soil my hands carrying your actual writing around –

ROCHESTER. He knows EXACTLY where to find us in a THOUSAND-ACRE PARK, arrives pat like a god in a Greek drama… Could not bear the threat, could you, of my writing a play –

ETHEREGE. A play? You don't think that counts as a play, do you?

ROCHESTER. You thin streak of piss. You prickless toad.

BARRY. I did it. (*Pause.*) I showed the King my copy the night before.

ROCHESTER. It seems I may have been mistaken, George, you know.

The MERRY GANG *await further apology but it's not forthcoming.*

And why might you have done that, Lizzie?

SACKVILLE *ushers the* MERRY GANG *out of the firing line.*

BARRY. I wanted to spare you the consequences of embarrassing the King in public.

ROCHESTER. The whole purpose was to embarrass him. So that he might, for once, be shown the truth about himself. Thanks to you I lost my time and effort writing that play.

BARRY. You have a divine talent. And yet you choose to see only what is base and mean. You are one-eyed. You look at humanity and you see the monkey, but you close your eyes to the angel. When I am on stage, I give wing to the angel, I let her soar over the rowdy Pit creatures until I have silenced them with the flapping of her wings. *That* is why they have begun to listen to me. Because when they have seen me, they leave the theatre with a larger idea of themselves and they become more noble in their daily lives. You show them to be a scrawny monkey in a shabby coat who shits and mounts its mate and they go on their way *meaner*.

ROCHESTER. I see them as they are and I portray what I see –

BARRY. You see differently. I know you do, for I have had you in the two o'clock dark when you have held me and, while we coupled, spoken thoughts richer than I have heard from any other man, and yet you are afraid to show this openly. When two o'clock is gone and you are the eleven-in-the-morning man, then you disavow that part of you that was so weak and gentle and must only rail and sneer. I would you had the courage to show the world the man I have seen, for did he but let himself shine, he would guide us all to a new and finer place.

ROCHESTER. That man is only for you, Lizzie, for only your eyes and voice can raise him from the dust. When he walks the world at eleven in the morning, he sees no sight that merits the love he finds in the darkness.

BARRY. I love you, John, but I do not love the part of you that determines always to show the worst of yourself, the worst of ourselves, the worst of everything.

ROCHESTER. Well, that is the part of me which is available.
  'I rise at eleven; I dine about two;
  I get drunk before seven and the next thing I do,
  I send for my whore, when for fear of the clap,
  I spend in her hand and I spew in her lap.
  I storm and I roar and I fall in a rage,
  And missing my lass, (*To* DOWNS.) I fall on my page;
  Then crop-sick, all morning I rail at my men,
  And in bed I lie yawning till eleven, again.'

BARRY *goes.* ROCHESTER *is stock-still.* DOWNS *approaches cautiously,* SACKVILLE *and* ETHEREGE *a little behind him.*

DOWNS. All right, Johnny?

ROCHESTER. What are we doing?

ETHEREGE. We're going to get a spot of supper. Charlie's treating us with his winnings –

ROCHESTER. I don't mean that, I mean WHAT ARE WE DOING?

SACKVILLE. Oh fuck, he's gone philosophical –

ETHEREGE. Johnny! I lost ten times what you did today.

SACKVILLE. Come on, let's make it an evening.

DOWNS. Yes, let's go on a freak and scare Epsom from its wits!

SACKVILLE (*retrieving a scrawled map from his pocket*). There is a whore here, gents, personally recommended by Mr Dryden himself, who glories in the name of Molly Noakes.

DOWNS. I am up her already!

ROCHESTER. Molly Noakes, the whore of Epsom. Such, gentlemen, is the offer which has been made to us at this point in our lives. All those in favour say 'Aye'.

SACKVILLE *and* DOWNS *say 'Aye'.*

Those against?

ETHEREGE. Nay.

SACKVILLE. George, you are becoming an old killjoy.

ETHEREGE. I want my dinner.

SACKVILLE. Won't roger Molly Noakes cos he wants his dinner.

DOWNS. You're becoming an OLD MAN, George.

SACKVILLE. Lead on. To the whorehouse!!

ALL. To the whorehouse!!

Quick blackout, then lights up. A door. It's now quite dark. The GANG look at the door.

DOWNS. This is it?

SACKVILLE. According to the Laureate.

DOWNS *hammers the door then pisses against it.*

DOWNS (*hammering*). MOLL-LY, MOLL-LY, MOLL-LY!!!

The door opens suddenly. A CONSTABLE *stands there.*
DOWNS *sprinkles on, aristocratically unconcerned.*

CONSTABLE. Gentlemen?

ROCHESTER. Where's Molly?

DOWNS. We want Molly and we want her fast.

CONSTABLE. Young man, you are pissing on my topboots.

DOWNS *finishes and buttons up.*

DOWNS. Yes, fellow, but you are only a common whorehouse
doorstepman and we are the cream of the country.

CONSTABLE. I am the Constable of the Watch.

SACKVILLE. You are what, sir?

CONSTABLE. I am the Constable and this is my house.

SACKVILLE. Dryden! Can't write a shag-map!

CONSTABLE. The honestest house in Epsom!

SACKVILLE. We are informed there is muff-bargain within
these portals.

CONSTABLE. No such thing, sir.

DOWNS. You are a rogue and a liar!

DOWNS *suddenly thumps the* CONSTABLE. ROCHESTER
immediately weighs in, followed by SACKVILLE.
ETHEREGE *dithers. The* CONSTABLE *hits the floor and
the three* GENTS *give him a kicking.*

ROCHESTER. Sorry, old chap. Did you slip?

SACKVILLE. Come all this way just to see our Molly!

ROCHESTER. Keep us from our Molly!

DOWNS. Cunt pretends he's a constable! Cunt-stable!

ALL. Cunt-stable, cunt-stable –

ETHEREGE. Johnny! Johnny!

Two GENTLEMEN OF THE WATCH *have emerged from the door. One carries a staff, the other a half-pike. They go for* DOWNS.

STAFF. All right, roarers, let's have you.

PIKE. Bright boy, start a tussle on our doorstep.

CONSTABLE. Hold him!

PIKE. Game gent, aren't you, sir?

STAFF. Every race day the same.

The GANG *back off. The* CONSTABLE *gets to his feet.*

CONSTABLE. Now then, gentlemen. I am the Constable of Epsom, these two fellows are of my watch and we would be pleased with any explanation you care to offer.

ETHEREGE. Ah! I do believe there has been a species of error.

CONSTABLE. And what would that error be, sir?

ROCHESTER *wishes to push the confrontation to the limit, but* ETHEREGE *is determined to make the peace.*

ROCHESTER. There has been no error –

ETHEREGE. Kind sir, I must protest that we are gentlemen, personal friends of His Majesty. This is the Earl of Dorset. And Middlesex. This, my Lord Rochester. I confess we have today attended the race meeting, and it will be immediately apparent to you that we have imbibed too freely of both grape and hop. Being erroneously persuaded that further entertainment could be encountered behind this door, my companions, perhaps overeagerly, pressed their aristocratic intentions to a point beyond the normal civility of our class. I do most deeply repent of any injury to any participant in this most regrettable interlude and assure everyone present that

we will make good such damage with our purses as well as
with our humble utterance.

ETHEREGE *distributes small bribes all round.*

ROCHESTER. Arsehole.

CONSTABLE. Gentleman, I know how the racing frenzy can
take hold of a fellow. Youthful spirits we shall say, youthful
spirits.

DOWNS. Dashed sorry, old fellow. Got borne away on the tide.

SACKVILLE. Most regrettable. Not too proud to shake hands
with an earl, sir?

CONSTABLE. Be honoured, sir.

All but ROCHESTER *shake the* CONSTABLE'*s hand.*

SACKVILLE. Here, have a drink with us.

SACKVILLE *produces a flask, has a nip and offers to the*
CONSTABLE, *who also takes one.*

CONSTABLE. All right. On your way, fellows.

The WATCH *hesitate a moment, then go.*

ETHEREGE. I am now seventy pound down on the day,
Charlie, and I'll be glad to take up your previous offer. Shall
we wend towards the inn?

DOWNS. Indeed we shall.

CONSTABLE. All you do, sir, is follow the road round to the
left –

Suddenly ROCHESTER *draws his sword.*

Help, ho!

ETHEREGE. Johnny, no!

ROCHESTER. You empty cullions, out of my way, I'll settle
him.

SACKVILLE. No!

DOWNS grabs ROCHESTER from behind.

ROCHESTER. Let me at him, let me at the sniveller!

DOWNS. Damn it, Johnny, we're all friends here!

SACKVILLE. Look, ho!

The WATCH *return. The* STAFFMAN *smashes at* DOWNS*'s skull.* DOWNS *falls.*

PIKE. Get the one with the sword!

DOWNS. Help me!

ROCHESTER, ETHEREGE *and* SACKVILLE *run off pursued by the* STAFFMAN. DOWNS *screams horribly.*

Where are you? Can't see, can't see!

DOWNS *flails. The* PIKEMAN *turns and runs him through.* DOWNS *cries out. The* STAFFMAN *comes back.*

STAFF. Made off. Cowards.

CONSTABLE. You went for the wrong one. Fellow had his sword out.

STAFF. I cudgelled him. Only to wound.

CONSTABLE. It's a wound all right.

PIKE. Smashed his skull.

DOWNS. Spark. Where is the spark? Where is –

DOWNS *is still.*

CONSTABLE. It's over with him.

PIKEMAN. Cowards.

Lights fade… Immediately a spot comes up on MALET.

MALET. When men are away for a long time, they change, not in themselves but in your mind. I heard first that he had gone to France, then why he had gone to France and I heard the word 'coward'. I had never thought his courage was in question, knowing he had fought at sea to good account. But

with the whisper of 'coward' I saw him differently.
Something in the foundations of my love shook. I sat with a
Bible on my lap in house too large for my needs and
wondered where he was.

Scene Ten – Attic

Doubtful morning light through a single attic window picks out
ROCHESTER. *He lies on a thin mattress in a mean little room*
in the East End of London. ALCOCK *comes in.*

ALCOCK. My lord! (*Pause.*) How goes it with you? I cannot
in all truth report that you look better. (*Pause.*) I have
haunted the apothecary's hoping to steal physic, but they are
watchful villains.

ROCHESTER. Where is Jane?

ALCOCK. Working the East End streets.

ROCHESTER. She has been absent many hours.

ALCOCK. Then perhaps we shall eat tonight.

ROCHESTER. She is a woman and not to be trusted.

ALCOCK. She has been steadfast in your hour of need.

ROCHESTER. You know I cannot abide loyalty.

ALCOCK. If you spit on hers you spit as well on mine.

ROCHESTER. I do. If this life in hiding gives you no
enjoyment, then depart.

ALCOCK. I shall see my service with you through to the end.

ROCHESTER. How insufferable. That you should degenerate
into the duteous servant… I have failed with you.

ALCOCK. You berate us. But without us you would die.

ROCHESTER. Alcock. Do you ever think on our Lord Jesus
Christ?

ALCOCK. My lord?

ROCHESTER. He was cast like me into the wilderness, he was scorned and reviled, he was, by one of his own followers, betrayed.

ALCOCK. I believe that in most respects, his life was of a different character from yours.

ROCHESTER. He would have brought Billy Downs back from the dead, do you not think?

ALCOCK. These are wandering thoughts, my lord.

ROCHESTER. I told him he had a dying countenance. Why does nobody listen?

JANE *comes on with bread and wine.*

Where have you been?

JANE. Turning minge into provender.

JANE *gives him wine.* ROCHESTER *guzzles.* ALCOCK *gnashes at the bread.*

Take at least a little bread.

ROCHESTER. I have now no stomach for food.

JANE. Take some!

JANE *feeds him bread.* ROCHESTER *dribbles it out.*

To think I once felt bullied by your appetites.

ROCHESTER (*drinking*). All are gone save one.

JANE. And that the one that beggars you the most. I took a wrong turning with you. I am too much in your company to be your fricatrice but too little in your mind to be more. For it is still full of Lizzie.

ROCHESTER. My mind will always be full of Lizzie.

JANE. Then you deserve what you shall receive.

CHARLES *comes in.*

CHARLES. Jane. Go to my coach. There is something there for you.

JANE *and* ALCOCK *go.*

ROCHESTER. I am unimpressed. It has taken you six weeks to find me.

CHARLES. Trivial though it may seem, I do have a country to run. Those Parliament bastards are trying to shaft me with a new bill which would exclude my successors from the throne. Subtle. Instead of chopping kings' heads off, you pick and choose the ones you want. It's my civil war. So, surprising though it may seem, you're not the first thing I think of when I wake up in the morning.

ROCHESTER. And why do I merit your attention now?

CHARLES. I wanted to tell you how well George's play is doing. *The Man of Mode* has taken the town.

ROCHESTER. So George is making money out of me.

CHARLES. He's a good writer.

ROCHESTER. *He's* a good writer, what am I then?

CHARLES. I don't know, John. What are you? Mr Etherege is packing out the Dorset Garden with you as the greatest spark on earth. But the town has you branded as a coward who leaves his friend to die in a brawl.

ROCHESTER. Alas.

CHARLES. People will stand for an awful lot, but they won't stand for coward.

ROCHESTER. All men would be cowards if they only had the courage.

CHARLES. The boy died. And you ran off –

ROCHESTER. I was pissed.

CHARLES. Well, of course you were.

ROCHESTER. I have to go too far, d'you see? I must always exceed or I don't feel like I'm alive.

CHARLES. And that's why my sundial got smashed and the great epic about my reign turns into a squalid little play about knobbing. And that's why Downs died. So you can feel alive.

ROCHESTER *drinks*.

ROCHESTER. The thing is this, Charlie, we expected so *much* of you. We thought you would *transform* everything just with your solemn and glittering presence. We wanted a Sun King. And when, after a few years, we saw it was just the same old caper, you asking Parliament for money, them telling you to piss off, you shutting down their shop, we were *bored* with all that. When we brought you back we thought 'Kings are divine,' that's what we missed, the godly touch. And finding that you didn't have it, that we could lose two wars to the Dutch, that London could be decimated with fire and pestilence, that we were still living on borrowed money, it wasn't what we'd signed up for. I can forgive you a great deal but I can't forgive you for not being a god.

CHARLES. You talk about your disappointment in me. It ain't a fraction of my disappointment in you.

ROCHESTER. I have lived my life in accordance with the values of your reign as my father would have wished.

CHARLES. Your father was a bigger piss-artist than you.

ROCHESTER. I never met him because he was constantly in exile trying to put you on the throne. I used to say to my mother: 'Why can't he be with us?' And she said: 'He has to be with the King.'

CHARLES. He didn't have to be with me. The reason why he wasn't with his family is the same reason you're not with your family now. He didn't like it –

ROCHESTER. That's not true.

CHARLES. He was too busy getting pissed somewhere to be bothered with you –

ROCHESTER. It isn't true –

CHARLES. I knew him and you didn't. I was restored to the throne in spite of his efforts. He was a useless prick.

ROCHESTER *launches himself at* CHARLES. CHARLES *draws his sword and levels it at* ROCHESTER'*s chest.*

Some moments. Then CHARLES *withdraws his sword.*

I thought about putting you in the Tower again. I even considered putting your head on a spike. But I've decided on something worse. I'm going to ignore you. I will no longer encourage in my breast any hope for you. I am condemning you to be you for the rest of your days.

JANE *comes on. She is much better dressed.*

You like your new dress?

JANE. You are very generous to me, Your Majesty.

CHARLES. Let us call it your reward. Now then, Jane, there is to be a ball at Greenwich tonight to celebrate the opening of the Observatory. And you shall be my dancing partner.

JANE. I shall always do what you command.

CHARLES. And I shall frequently command you.

CHARLES *and* JANE *dance off together.* ROCHESTER *is left alone.*

A moment. Then the lights fade. ETHERGE *comes on.*

ETHEREGE. It was the summer when everyone walked at the pace I chose. While Dryden strained at his iambs and my Lord Rochester thumped the head of his muse against a wall called Lizzie, I simply wrote down what I saw. And when the Dorset Gardens Theatre put my play on, it became, for a few hot months, the centre of the civilised world.

Scene Eleven – Backstage with Barry

Backstage at the Dorset Gardens Theatre during a performance of The Man of Mode. *The house is rocking with laughter.*
LUSCOMBE *stands with the prompt copy.* BARRY *is coming offstage.*

LUSCOMBE (*to offstage*). Mr Harris!

BARRY. Whose idea was it to employ Mr Smith?

LUSCOMBE. Where is Mr Harris?

    LUSCOMBE *exits.*

BARRY. If he lisps much more he'll bite his tongue off.

    LUSCOMBE *returns dragging* HARRIS. *He holds a small pie.* BARRY *goes onstage.*

LUSCOMBE. You had four minutes, Mr Harris. That is enough time to buy a pie. It is enough time to eat a pie. But it is not enough time to buy *and* eat a pie.

HARRIS. I'm here, ain't I?

LUSCOMBE. The fine for nearly missing an entrance is one pie. On you go!

    LUSCOMBE *shoves* HARRIS *onstage. She takes a bite from the pie, a small victory in a day of defeats. Some moments, then* ETHEREGE *and* ROCHESTER *come on.* ROCHESTER *walks with difficulty.*

ETHEREGE. Molly! Brought the Earl in to gawp at me triumph.

LUSCOMBE. Authors have a place, Mr Etherege. It is in the garret. I do not like them cluttering up my theatre.

ETHEREGE. It ain't your theatre –

LUSCOMBE. While the curtain is up, Mr Etherege, it is my theatre and to anyone who balks at my slightest whim I will take a meat-axe.

ROCHESTER. Oh, Moll, don't give us your iron mask, we were ever your chums.

LUSCOMBE. In my profession there are no chums, there are only degrees of enemy.

ETHEREGE (*whispers*). Lizzie won't see him. Won't see Johnny. This is the only way.

ETHEREGE *introduces a half-crown coin into the conversation.*

LUSCOMBE. Money don't buy this, Mr Etherege. Do you not see? This is my life.

ETHEREGE (*withdrawing it*). Sorry, Moll. Just five minutes.

LUSCOMBE (*relenting*). I don't want her upset. She comes off in ten lines.

ROCHESTER. I love theatres. They remind me of ships, great rocking galleons floating into battle. I could have written a splendid play, you know, had it not been beneath me.

ETHEREGE. Yes.

An enormous laugh from the house.

ROCHESTER. Oh, George, you've done it. But you know what they're laughing at? They're not laughing at your wit, they're laughing at mine.

ETHEREGE. Don't deceive yourself.

ROCHESTER. What?

ETHEREGE. You couldn't have written a splendid play. You don't have the gift. But I have caught the scent and flavour of our age and set it down for all time. *The Man of Mode*. You didn't write it because you couldn't.

ROCHESTER. I didn't write it because I was too busy living it. I am the age, I don't want to be its chronicler.

ETHEREGE. You were right about Lizzie though. The finest actress on our stage.

ROCHESTER. I love her, you know.

ETHEREGE. Love? 'Love gilds us over and makes us show fine things to each other for a time, but soon the gold wears off and then again the native brass appears.'

BARRY comes offstage. She looks around.

(*Bowing.*) Lizzie.

BARRY (*to* LUSCOMBE). What is *he* doing here?

LUSCOMBE. Don't blame me. I am not a lord. I am someone for whom good fortune means a free pie.

LUSCOMBE eats and buries herself in the prompt copy.

ETHEREGE. John. I'll see you after. I'll be in Long's.

ROCHESTER. Very well. Or Lockett's?

ETHEREGE. Long's.

ETHEREGE slips away towards the stage door. An edgy moment. ROCHESTER sits on a costume hamper, drinking claret from a bottle.

BARRY (*to* ROCHESTER). Have you seen this play?

ROCHESTER. I saw it yesterday.

BARRY. And what did you think?

ROCHESTER. You don't care what I think.

BARRY. If you have only come to sulk –

She turns to go.

ROCHESTER. You're brilliant in it. I thought… I thought you only had the tragic gift. But you were light and larky and true. And you made me laugh. I had a couple of notes. I wrote them down somewhere.

He searches his pockets for a moment, then stops.

What's the point? Even if I give them to you, you won't take any notice, will you?

BARRY. No. I won't.

ROCHESTER. But I taught you once. I did teach you, didn't I?

BARRY. You taught me to rehearse, to repeat a part over and over again so that I was so familiar with it I was free to act.

ROCHESTER. I won a bet off George over you, a hundred guineas. What the devil became of that money?

BARRY. It went the way of all the other money.

ROCHESTER. Yes.

> ROCHESTER *drinks, finishing the bottle.*

It went into bottles and I threw them into the sea with messages inside, and somewhere in years to come, people will pick the messages out and read them aloud and wonder.

> HARRIS *comes offstage dressed as Dorimant.* LUSCOMBE *helps him with his costume change.*

So, Mr Harris, you portray the merry Lord Dorimant, do you? May I ask you how it feels to be me?

LUSCOMBE. Mr Harris has a quick change and you will let him be.

ROCHESTER. I am nature and you are art, let us see how we compare.

HARRIS. I have one minute.

> ROCHESTER *grasps* HARRIS *by the wrist and presents the pair of them to* BARRY.

ROCHESTER. I don't half feel a jolly gaping gulf between the ideal and the real. Here we have him, your Restoration Gent. He has not pissed his breeches today and there are no creatures in his periwig. He can walk in a more or less straight line for over two hundred yards without falling on his face and retching. He has a sparkish spring to his boots and conveys the overwhelming impression of a few hundred pound under his mattress and a rising fountain of blood in his cods. Now look you upon this picture and on this. He has not washed, he cannot walk and he most certainly will not be able to raise either the price of a dinner or his own pintle. But he can drink. Which of these would you prefer to see on the stage?

HARRIS. I must be got into my nightgown.

> ROCHESTER *releases* HARRIS. LUSCOMBE *helps him into his costume.*

ROCHESTER. This is what I envy in you stage people. The notion that something HAS TO BE and within the next few seconds. You make time seem so important. I must change my clothes NOW, I must make my entrance NOW. But that is not what life is, it isn't a succession of urgent NOWS it's a listless trickle of 'Why should I's?' That's why nothing that happens on a stage is true. Do you understand that, Mr Harris?

LUSCOMBE. You're on.

> HARRIS *goes onstage.* LUSCOMBE *gives* ROCHESTER *a hard look, but decides not to take him on.*

You have five minutes only, Mrs Barry.

BARRY. Yes, Molly. (*To* ROCHESTER.) You used to love the theatre.

ROCHESTER. I still love theatres, I just despise what happens inside them. It is absurd, the way the whole farrago engages people so.

BARRY. It's a world, like any other – the law courts or the counting house. If you engage in life, you engage necessarily in some absurdity.

ROCHESTER. I want you to leave the theatre.

> *Pause.*

BARRY. It is my livelihood. In an uncertain world.

ROCHESTER. But it needs not be. There is one here who could provide for you better.

BARRY. I see no one.

> ROCHESTER *stands and speaks to her, formally but very naturally, without embroidering the text.*

ROCHESTER. 'Leave this gaudy gilded stage,
　　From custom more than use frequented,
　　Where fools of either sex and age
　　Crowd to see themselves presented.

　　To love's theatre, the bed,
　　Youth and beauty fly together,
　　And act so well it may be said
　　The laurel there was due to either.

　　'Twixt strifes of love and war,
　　The difference lies in this:
　　When neither overcomes,
　　Love's triumph greater is.'

BARRY. 'When neither overcomes.' That isn't the truth about love. It is invariably a war and there is always a victor and a vanquished.

ROCHESTER. I don't want you for a mistress, Lizzie. I want you for a wife.

BARRY. You have a wife.

ROCHESTER. There are ways of proceeding. For an intimate of the King, such a thing may be accomplished.

BARRY. Oh, the King, your good friend. What strange bedfellows this storm brings you!

ROCHESTER. You chide me that I have never engaged in life. Well, I mean to begin, and I would have my divorce dispatched that I may dedicate myself to you.

BARRY. And money?

ROCHESTER. I still have money.

BARRY. You have your wife's money.

ROCHESTER. A fellow such as I can always lay hands on money.

BARRY. A fellow like you can always spend it.

ROCHESTER. YOU KNOW WHAT I MEAN!!

BARRY. You have no understanding, do you? You have comprehended – just – that I am tired of being your mistress and your solution is to conscript me into becoming your wife. It is not being a mistress I am tired of, John. I am tired of you. I do not wish to be your wife. I do not wish to be anyone's wife. I wish to continue being the creature I am. I am no Nell Gwyn, I will not give up the stage as soon as a king or a lord has seen me on it and, wishing me to be his and his alone, will then pay a fortune to keep me off it. I am not the sparrow you picked up in the roadside, my love. London walks into this theatre to see *me* – not George's play nor Mr Betterton. They want me and they want me over and over again. And when people desire you in such a manner, then you can envisage a *lifetime* of money amassed through your own endeavours. That is riches. 'Leave this gaudy, gilded stage.' You're right, this stage is gilded. It is gilded with my future earnings. And I will not trade those for a dependency on you. I will not swap my certain glory for your undependable love.

ROCHESTER. Even if I were to give you children?

BARRY. It makes no difference. I have your child in my belly at this moment.

ROCHESTER. You are carrying our child?

BARRY. I will have it this summer while the theatres are closed and by the start of the season I will be flat enough to play Desdemona in a nightgown.

ROCHESTER. But this is not only your child –

BARRY. You have children already. What difference do they make to you, what difference would another bring?

LUSCOMBE. Mrs Barry. Two minutes please.

ROCHESTER. This is not like the other children. This is the child of our passion –

BARRY. Different, yes, in its bastardy –

ROCHESTER. Passion which would confirm it a child of hope. My other children were born of despair, conceived in a country marriage bed. When I bred them, I placed no value on my life, no importance on human life at all. When I met you I was, in that instant, delivered from still life, delivered from the ice of my own soul. You dragged me in from the edges of the world to eat the meat I had mocked when I saw it spread on other men's tables. And I ate it and knew it to be good. But now you send me away hungry from the table and I cannot go back to the region whence I came. I CANNOT FORGIVE YOU FOR TEACHING ME TO LOVE LIFE.

BARRY. If I taught you that – and I confess I never set out so to do – then it was a good lesson for it is a thing that can never be learned too late. I thank you for what start you gave me on the stage. But, John, if I have taught you what you say, then our account is settled. Your lesson to me was my livelihood, and mine to you was life itself. We have no need to meet again.

ROCHESTER. Lizzie –

BARRY. If you are in London and have half a crown in your pocket, you may see me there. (*The stage.*) For the rest I hope I shall be always in your heart and sometime in your thoughts but never in your debt.

BARRY *adjusts her costume, looks in the mirror held out for her, nods to* LUSCOMBE *and, without turning back, goes onstage.* LUSCOMBE *and* ROCHESTER *watch. There is much laughter at her entrance.*

ROCHESTER. She has such life in her. That's what they come for.

LUSCOMBE. I have never seen the like, not in all my years at this. I watch her every night. It is always the same and yet always different. And when she goes off, I do not live until I see her on again.

And indeed LUSCOMBE *turns all her attention on the stage, mouthing the words to* BARRY*'s performance.*

ROCHESTER. That's right, Molly. We do not live. We do not live.

ROCHESTER *watches for a moment, then goes.*

Lights fade to blackout.

Scene Twelve – Husband and Wife

Immediately lights come up on ALCOCK.

ALCOCK. The discerning traveller, having a mind to visit Adderbury, takes the road through Watford, spends the night in Aylesbury and, after an early start, is sitting down to lunch at his destination, four miles south of Banbury. There is, however, another way, not the way of the discerning traveller, but what I shall call the Arsehole Way. Journeying in the Arsehole manner, you stop at an inn after three minutes on the road and find yourself still within its precincts at one o'clock in the morning. You then sink into a stupor until dawn, at which point you fall to shouting at your minions and ride like the clappers, until, a mile short of Aston Clinton, a wheel works loose and you have to walk to an inn in search of a blacksmith. He not appearing immediately, you take handsomely to the company and fall into a drunken stupor again. You do not wake till early evening but then cover the final thirty miles at a mouth-frothing velocity and tumble, more dead than alive, into an empty house whose owner and servants have long ago taken to their beds. We did not take the way of the discerning traveller.

The space has become the dark dining room of ROCHESTER's *own house. It's the middle of the night.* ALCOCK *comes on with a lit candelabra which he puts down on a table. He takes* ROCHESTER's *coat.*

ROCHESTER. Bring me some wine.

ALCOCK. It's late, sir, I'll have to wake the cellarman.

ROCHESTER. Break down the door, fool.

ALCOCK. It is oak, my lord.

ROCHESTER. There is an axe mounted on the lintel of the doorway opposite, my father put it there for emergencies.

ALCOCK. I believe the emergencies he envisaged were of a more Cromwellian nature.

ROCHESTER. Do not cross me!

ALCOCK. I can't do it.

ROCHESTER. How I hate the country! You cannot even get a drink in your own house.

ROCHESTER throws his empty brandy bottle on the floor. MALET comes in.

Elizabeth! Get the servants up at once, we have ridden all night, we need drink.

MALET immediately throws a heavy bunch of keys onto the table. Some moments, then ALCOCK picks them up and goes off to the cellars.

Thank you.

Pause.

We set out in good time but we were delayed. Can one find a blacksmith within a thirty-mile radius who understands his trade, NO!!

Pause.

And the roads, it goes without saying are a disgrace.

Pause.

The poplars we planted on my last visit. Are they thriving?

Pause.

Mr Rose, the King's gardener, presented him with a pineapple the other day. I do not altogether approve. Pineapples, growing in England, it argues too much the final triumph of art over nature.

ROCHESTER *breaks down and cries.* MALET *stands looking at him.*

MALET. John. I am ever your last resort. When your mistress has kicked you into the street and no innkeeper in London will give you credit, when you are wasted with disease and the last whore in Covent Garden refuses to attend to you, then and only then do you come to me.

ROCHESTER. That's not true.

MALET. Have I been so remiss in my wedding vows that you run so assiduously from the woman whose company you should most fervently pursue?

ROCHESTER. My most neglected wife, till you are a much-respected widow I find you will scarce be a contented woman, and to say no more than the plain truth I endeavour so fairly to do you that last good service that none but the most impatient would be dissatisfied.

MALET. Your meaning is that you are trying your hardest to make me a widow.

ROCHESTER. No man ever endeavoured harder.

MALET. I don't want you to die, I want you to live and live differently.

ROCHESTER. I have been able to bear many things, even the pain of the stone which keeps me from rest, but the worst pain of all has been to hear you complaining but never to confess what part of you is hurt.

MALET. It is all too clear what has been my hurt. It has been your persistent business to be absent from my hearth, my board and my bed.

ROCHESTER. If I have been absent, well, I have had business, and even then you have been constantly in my thoughts, as witness the spate of letters I have sent you.

MALET. If there was anything that ever troubled me when I was lucky enough to receive a letter from you it was this: that you would never name a time when I might hope to see you. I

have never known why you did this to me. Wherever you are,
I never know when you will find it in your heart to leave that
place and come home to me. Consider with yourself whether
this be a reasonable way of proceeding. Let me know what I
am to expect. I can fulfil my marriage vows to you, but only if
I know where you will be and what schemes are in your head.

ALCOCK *is back, bearing two open bottles of wine.*

ALCOCK. My lord.

ROCHESTER *immediately snatches a bottle and drinks.*

MALET. I will take the other.

ALCOCK. My lady.

ALCOCK *is surprised but hands over the bottle to* MALET,
who drinks from it.

MALET. Thank you, Alcock.

ALCOCK *hands the keys to* MALET *and goes.*

ROCHESTER. Lizzie, I do not wish to drive you onto the path
of intemperance.

MALET. Why not? If it is good for you, why, is it not good for
me too?

ROCHESTER. It is not good for me.

MALET. It is not good for you?

ROCHESTER. I am troubled with the stone. When I pass water
I am in agonies, in the morning I –

MALET. Why then do you pursue the path?

ROCHESTER. Of intemperance?

MALET. Yes, why? When were you last a sober man?

ROCHESTER. I?

Some moments. ROCHESTER *poses the question to himself
seriously.* MALET *stands watching him, holding the open
bottle.*

It was… No, no. It was three years ago. No, four? Five?

MALET. And are you not, John, a rational kind of man? Has not your intellect been praised on all sides?

ROCHESTER. It has.

MALET. So a wise man, a man of intellect, knowing that something is doing him harm, is wracking him with agues and diseases, and that five years of constant work at this practice have rendered his body feeble and his spirit low, what would this wise man, this man of intellect do?

Pause.

ROCHESTER. You seek to trap me like a cunning lawyer.

MALET. What would he do?

ROCHESTER. He would desist.

MALET. He would desist. And those he loved, would they not show their love by beseeching him to desist?

ROCHESTER. It is not so simple –

MALET. Would such not be fair sign and token of their love?

Pause.

ROCHESTER. It would.

Silence. Then MALET slowly inverts the bottle and starts to pour the claret on the floor. ROCHESTER makes a lunge to prevent her but then, transfixed, watches. Halfway through the bottle, MALET stops.

MALET. Have you known me waste anything before?

ROCHESTER. No.

MALET. And why do I waste this now?

Pause.

ROCHESTER. So that it does not waste me.

MALET. So that it does not waste you.

MALET recommences pouring. ROCHESTER makes another lunge to stop her. He can only hold himself back by

taking a drink from his own bottle, which he does. MALET
pours until the bottle is empty. She looks at ROCHESTER.
ROCHESTER *begins to choke on the wine, spitting it out
onto the floor. He stares at the wine on the floor at his feet.
Some moments. Then he takes the remains of his bottle and
begins to pour it on the floor. Close to the end of the bottle,
he repents and tries to bring the bottle to his lips.* MALET *is
quickly beside him to prevent this. She holds him. The bottle
rolls onto the floor. She holds him while he sobs.*

I have heard men say that the Devil, God save me, is in you.
If that be so, I know how he made his entrance.

ROCHESTER. I have never ceased to love you. But I have not
loved life.

MALET. Shush, shush, you have strived to be happy.

ROCHESTER. I would now write all my follies in a book
dedicated to you and publish it to all the world.

MALET. Come, John, it is too late for talk of that kind. Come
now to bed.

ROCHESTER *sinks onto* MALET*'s breast. She holds him.
He is quite still – asleep or dead. A light comes up on*
ALCOCK.

ALCOCK. After I left his employ, I no longer had the
enjoyment of life for which he had hired me. And when the
end came, the manner of his departing was not credited.

ALCOCK*'s light goes out. Light up on* SACKVILLE.

SACKVILLE. My lord had never believed in God because of
Mr Wyndham at the Battle of Bergen. The night before the
engagement, my lord and Mr Wyndham, being possessed of
a premonition of death, made a solemn bond that if either
was killed he should return to the survivor with tidings of
the afterlife.

Lights up on the DOWNS *actor: his face is bloody.*

DOWNS. Where is the spark? Where is the spark?

SACKVILLE. The next day a cannonball carried away Mr
Wyndham's belly. He not appearing from the grave, my lord
thenceforward turned his face from God.

DOWNS. Where is the spark?

SACKVILLE. What a pity we have to die at the end of our lives
when our intellects are too feeble to repel the religious
fellows who creep upon us in our troubled hours. My lord
held the soul to be merely a function of the body until he
stopped drinking. When you have enfeebled yourself with
liquor and the body withers, it seems it is more attractive to
think the opposite – that the body will drop away and the
soul will soar.

DOWNS. Where is the spark?

Light up on BARRY. *She speaks to the audience.*

BARRY. 'He charmed the tenderest virgins to delight
And with his style did fiercest blockheads fright
Some beauties here, I see,
Though now demure, have felt his powerful charms
And languished in the circle of his arms.
But for ye fops, his satire reached ye all,
And under his lash your whole vast herd did fall.
Oh fatal loss! That mighty spirit's gone!
Alas! His too great heat went out too soon.'

BARRY*'s light goes out. Light up on* ROCHESTER.

ROCHESTER. When I poured away the last bottle of wine I
saw the blood of Christ streaming onto the floor and it took
all my effort not to throw myself on my face and guzzle. But
I desisted and my mind cleared and I made an inventory of
my life and found much wanting: injuries to divers people:
want of attention to my affairs: a lifetime spitting in the face
of God, and I knew I was to be cast down. I had long ago
discarded the layer of formal politeness with which we
negotiate the world, but now I had to wade through the
slough of my licentiousness until I found level ground
underfoot, a ground of true sensibility and love of Christ.

Now I gaze upon a pinhead and see angels dancing. Well. Do you like me now? Do you like me now?

Blackout.

End.

MUSIC

Mickey Gallagher

SIGNIOR DILDO

You la-dies all of merry Eng-land Who have
been to kiss the Duch-ess'-s hand
Pray did you late-ly ob-serve in the show A

A Nick Hern Book

The Libertine first published in Great Britain as a paperback original in 1994 by Nick Hern Books Limited, The Glasshouse, 49a Goldhawk Road, London W12 8QP

This new edition published in 2014 in association with the Citizens Theatre, Glasgow

Designed and typeset by Nick Hern Books, London
Printed in Great Britain by CPI Group (UK) Ltd

A CIP catalogue record for this book is available from the British Library

ISBN   978 1 84842 387 9